AF260862

Devour:

Art & Lit Canada

is dedicated to the Canadian voice.

www.WetInkBooks.com

ISSN 2561-1321

Issue 015

Devour

Art & Lit Canada

Find some of Canada's
finest authors, photographers and artists
featured in every issue.

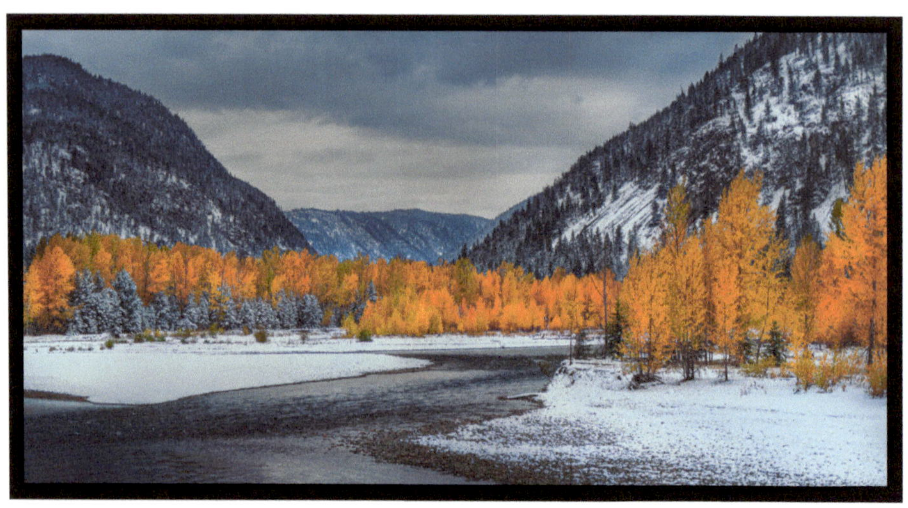

Cover Photograph by Matt Shannon
matt@mattshannon.ca
https://www.mattshannon.ca/

The mission of *Devour:*
Art and Lit Canada

is to promote Canadian culture by
bringing world-wide readers some of the best
Canadian literature, art and photography.

Devour: Art and Lit Canada
ISSN 2561-1321
Issue 015
Winter 2022 / 23

5 Greystone Walk Drive
Unit 408
Toronto, Ontario, Canada, M1K 5J5
DevourArtAndLitCanada@gmail.com

Poetry Editor – Bruce Kauffman
Review Editor – Shane Joseph
Photography Curator – Olaf Dijkstra
Front and Back Cover Feature Photographer –
Matt Shannon

Editor-in-Chief – Richard M. Grove
Layout and Design – Richard M. Grove

Welcome to this 15th issue of Devour: Art & Lit Canada. As usual we are bringing you some of Canada's most talented writers, poets and photographers.

We hope you will tell your international readers about this all Canadian Magazine.

We are looking for a prose editor to provide one or two short stories or excerpts, or micro prose or novel exerpts with a short intro for the Summer and Winter issues.

We welcome Olaf Dijkstra as our Photography Curator - see page 30. He chose the feature photographer Matt Shannon - see page

See you between the pages.
Richard Grove otherwise know to friends as Tai

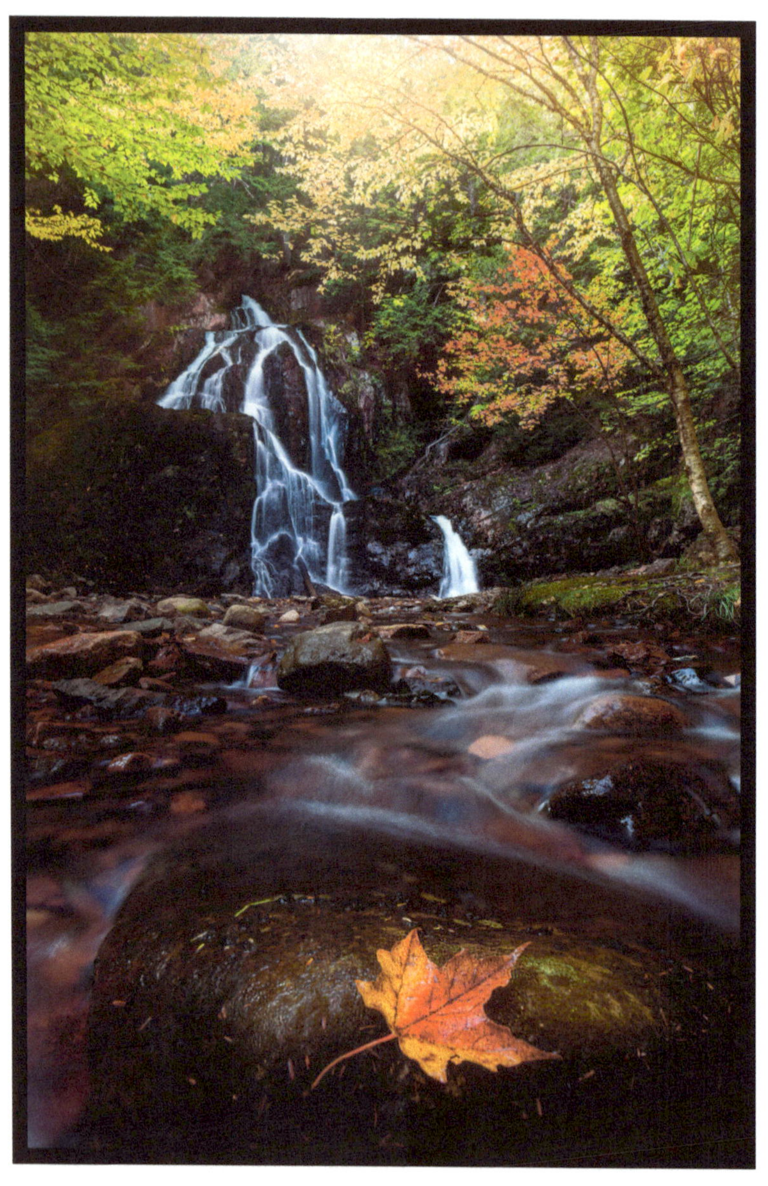

Matt Shannon

Devour
Art& Lit Canada

Content

Features:

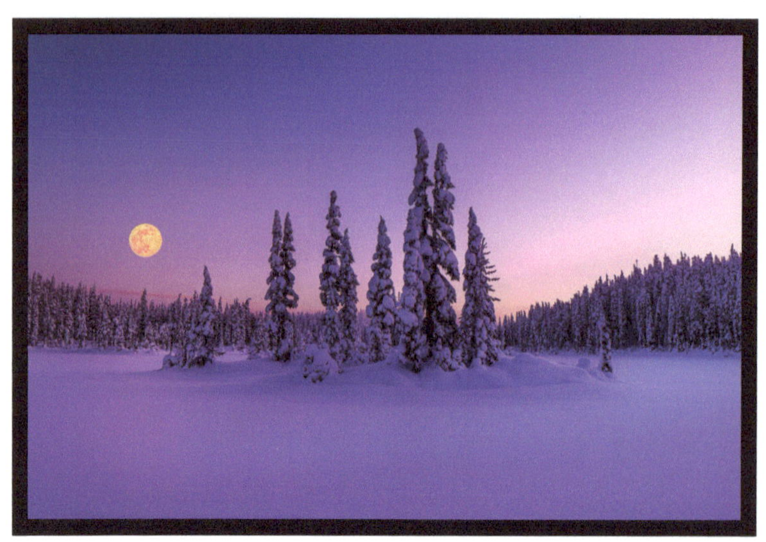

Moon over trees – Matt Shannon

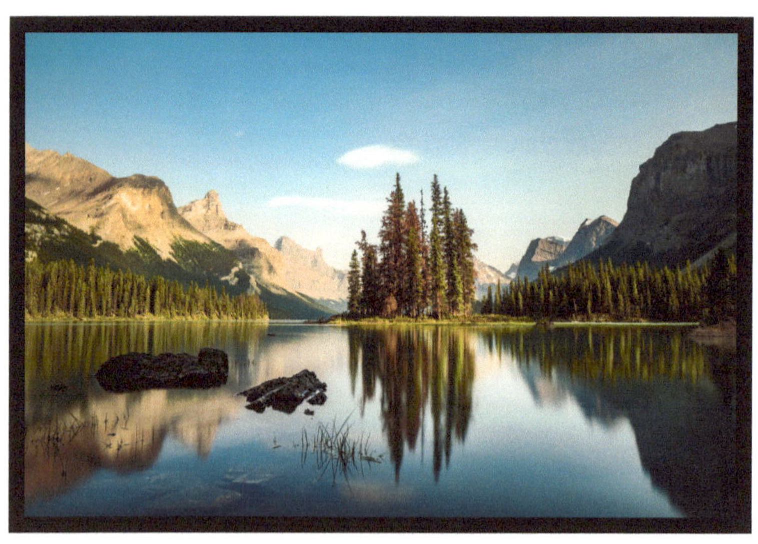

Spirit bay – Matt Shannon

Feature Photographer, Matt Shannon

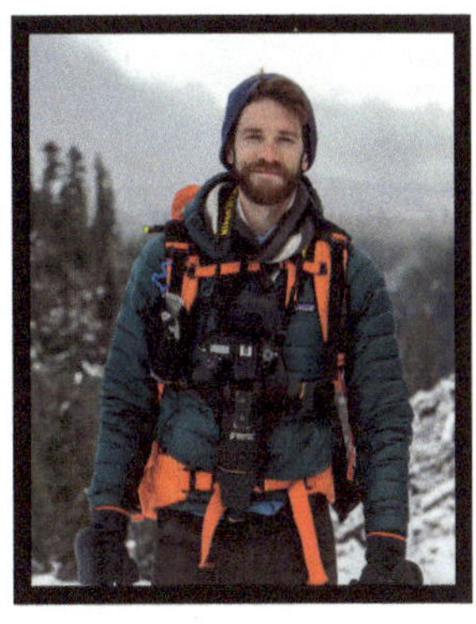

Matt Shannon is an inspired nature and landscape photographer living on Vancouver Island. His images have captured an international audience and his artwork hangs in homes around the world. He has developed a keen eye for detail and a passion for striking images. He is an enthusiastic teacher and hosts regular workshops aimed at inspiring and equipping photographers.

From a young age Matt Shannon was captivated with the wild world around him. He grew up in a small town in New Brunswick where he would practice his survival skills camping in the dense forest. After high school Matt leapt out into the world, falling in love with traveling. He explored South America, Asia and India and drove across North America 9 times. It was his exploration of new places that first inspired his love of photography. Matt loved that the lens allowed him to share these new worlds with his friends and family back home.

Matt still remembers his first trip to Vancouver Island over a decade ago when he spent the night on Mystic Beach on the Juan de Fuca Trail. He fell in love with the rugged coastline, massive trees and the endless adventures Vancouver Island holds and has called the Island home ever since.

Matt's photography is the product of his adventuresome heart - it's the physical representation of his love for striking landscapes and beautiful natural creations. Today Matt continues to explore the west coast and capture compelling images to share.

Matt's fine art landscape prints can be found in his Online Store. Please feel free to contact Matt directly about custom printing options.

Matt Shannon: matt@mattshannon.ca
URL: MattShannon.ca
Cell: (250)-858-1679
Facebook: https://www.facebook.com/mattshannonphotography
Instagram: https://www.instagram.com/matt_shannon_photography/
Linkedin: https://www.linkedin.com/in/matt-shannon-397a23116/
Youtube: https://www.youtube.com/@MattShannonPhoto

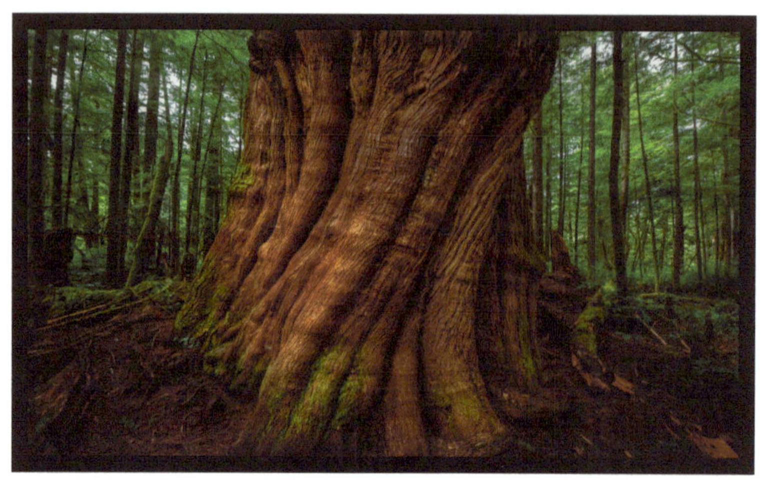

Twisted Tree – Matt Shannon

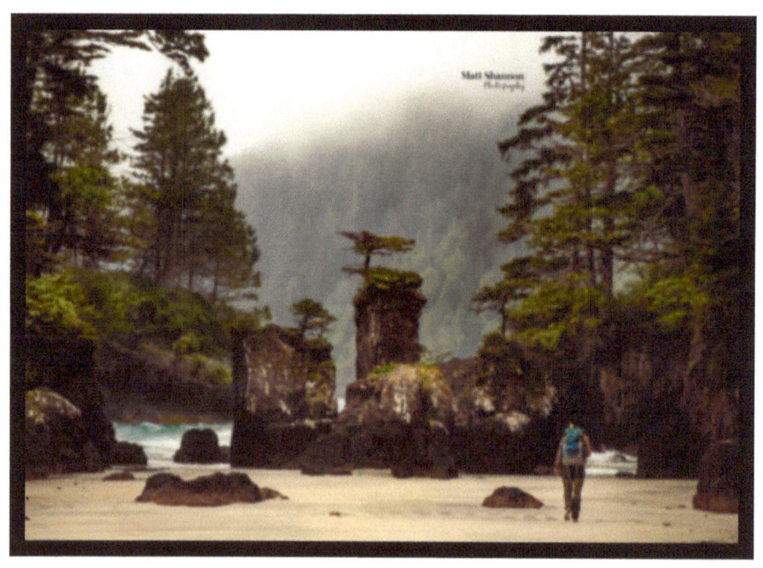

Beach – Matt Shannon

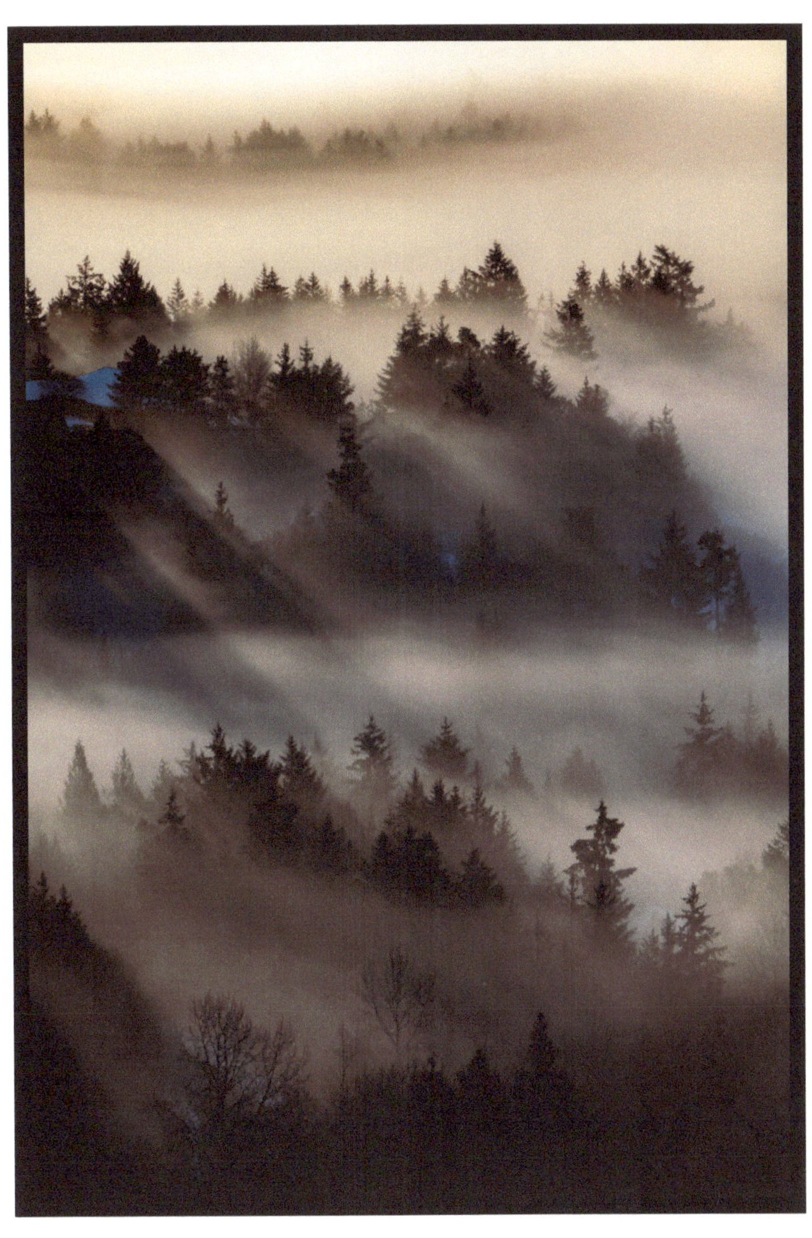

Trees and Clouds – Matt Shannon

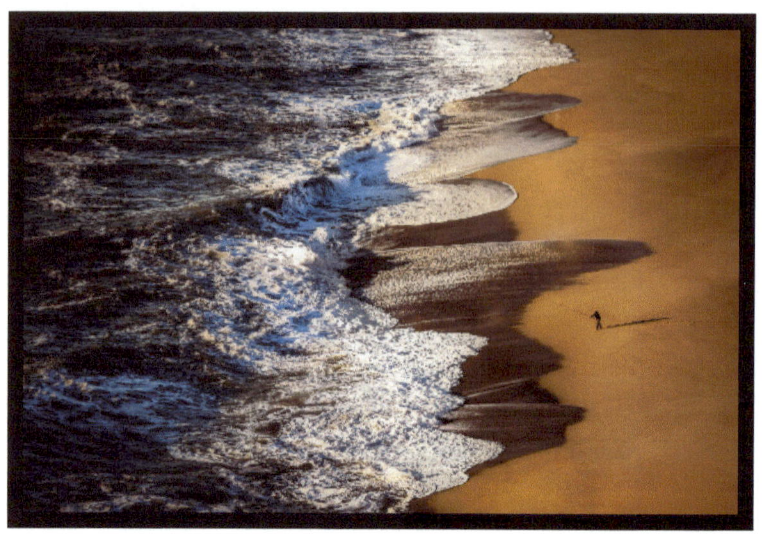

Fisher Beach – Matt Shannon

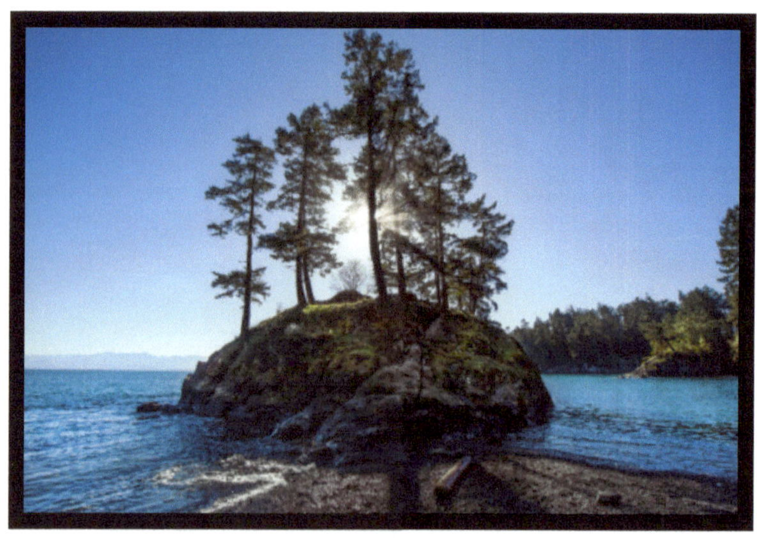

Island in the Sun – Matt Shannon

CANADA in REVIEW

Review Editor
SHANE JOSEPH

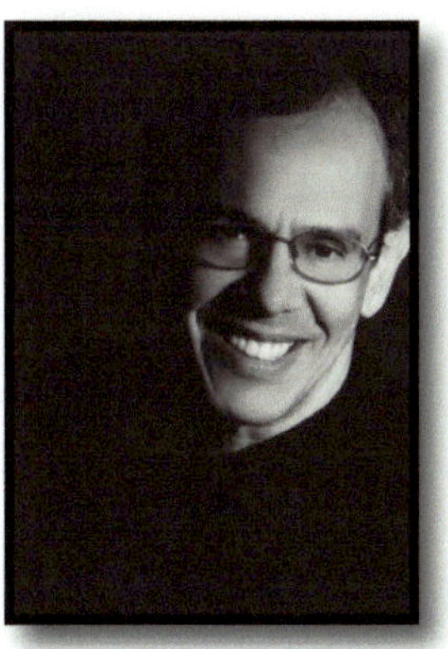

Book Editor's Note:

This collection of reviews focusses on books with a lot of local faire, and when I say "local," it's close to my home: Northumberland County, Ontario, where we recently concluded an arts festival of over 40 events including literature, theatre, film, music, dance, photography and other arts, celebrating the cultural richness of this region. Therefore, I thought local samples would be appropriate at this time.

Thorneside Stories typifies the goings-on in a small Ontario town, replete with secrets, tragedies, eccentric characters, and ribald humour. ***The Last Secret*** takes us back to the 19th century in the same locale when a courageous woman tries to run a dairy while being hounded by overbearing men who think she does not have the right stuff. And in ***The Many Secrets***, we are treated to "poetry that paints" imagery, memory, and mood of our pastoral surroundings. A late entry, ***Shame to Shine***, a collection of poetry that transcends the cruel legacy of domestic violence and generational trauma, by Indigenous writer Cher Obediah whose roots stretch into the Alderville First Nation, rounds up our local serving.

Moving beyond the borders of Northumberland, we travel to Morocco and Egypt in the novel ***In Love With The Night***, to conclude the mysterious and mystical events that took place in its prequel, ***The Way Things Fall***, which was also reviewed here a year ago.

Finally, we take a look at an enigmatic figure, Mary Welsh Hemingway, and her attempts to live with the tempestuous ego of a literary legend in ***Hemingway's Widow***.

Great books, all of them, for this winter season.

Shane Joseph

Title: ***Hemingway's Widow –***
The Life and Legacy of Mary Welsh Hemingway

Author: **Timothy Christian**

ISBN: 9781643138831

Number of Pages: 458

Published Year: 2022

Reviewed by **Gail M. Murray**

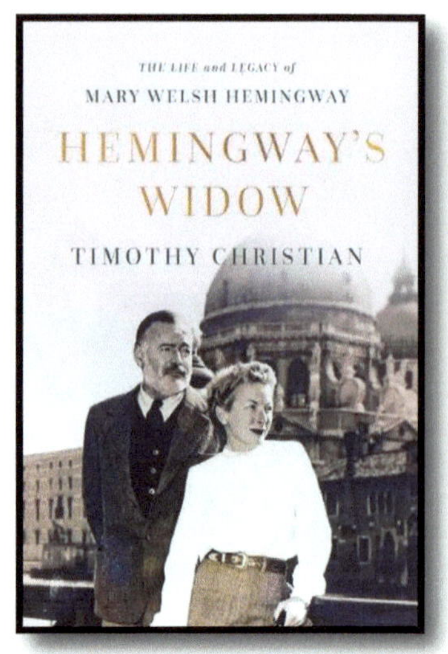

Canadian biographer and former law professor, Christian's meticulous archival research interviews people who knew Mary and quotes from her memoir, *How It Was*, striving to paint an honest portrait and present a fresh analysis of her complex life. It includes Stoneback's preface, extensive footnotes, and a bibliography of six pages. The bulk of the book delineates her relationship with her famous husband. The initial five chapters that focus only on her, prove the most insightful and are an enchanting read about the petite blonde's bold spirit. How delightful, singing Irish ballads along with her father as they sailed The Northland, delivering timber from the Minnesota woods, and later listening to Chopin and Hamlet as he fosters her writing.

Mary succeeds as a journalist writing for Time Magazine during The London Blitz. Though married to Australian journalist, Noel Monks, Mary juggled relationships with General Bob McClure and handsome American novelist, Ian Shaw, author of *The Young Lions*, whom she described as "the best lay in Europe."

Enter Hemingway, writing for Colliers, who pursues her relentlessly. She had doubts. She found Hemingway's self-absorption unattractive, but he was exciting and adventurous. Though Shaw was her first choice; she agreed to marry Hemingway. This one choice changed her life dramatically for good or ill. Through countless examples Christian describes their volatile, co-dependent pairing. The drama increases as they move to *La Finca Vigia* in Cuba. Hemingway insists she give up her career and become his emotional anchor, supporting his creative power. His charisma dominates their social life as her personality melts away. Drinking to excess, this Pulitzer Prize winner/Nobel Laureate is a narcissist and a cruel bully. Much of the book exposes their back-and-forth relationship. Many times she thought to leave, yet she loved him and the lifestyle.

Christian creates sympathy for Mary. Her Madison Avenue penthouse apartment recreates *La Finca Vigia,* her home, with the paintings *The Guitar Player* by Juan Gris and Joan Miro's *The Farm*, with taxidermy of leopard, lion and gazelle, a zebra carpet in the living room, and Waldo Peirce's 1929 portrait of thirty-one-year-old Ernest hung over her bed. After seventeen years of marriage, she lived surrounded by mementoes of her years with him. Following Hemingway's death, the book skews off course into a series of separate essays as Mary tenaciously protects his legacy. I wonder, what if Shaw had left his wife for her? I'm intrigued to read her memoir.

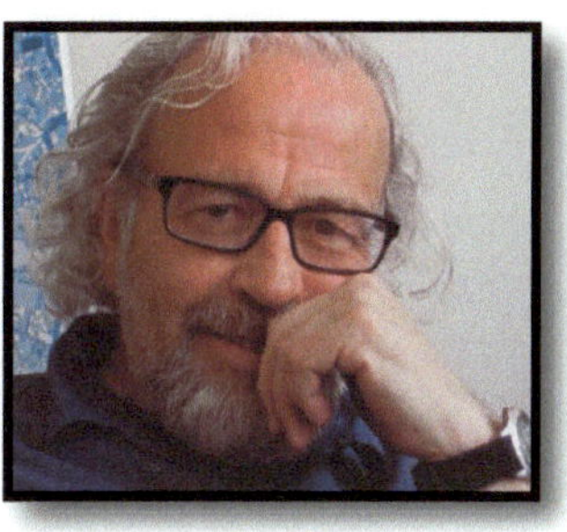

Timothy Christian graduated as a Commonwealth Scholar from King's College, Cambridge. During a varied legal career, he served as a law professor and Dean at the Faculty of Law at the University of Alberta and a visiting professor in Japan and Taiwan. Christian read *A Moveable Feast* in the cafes of Aix-en-Provence when he was a young man studying French. Realizing that no one had written deeply about Mary Welsh Hemingway, Christian began researching her story—and discovered a woman vital to Hemingway's art. Christian is married to a lawyer and abstract artist, Kathryn Dykstra, and lives in a Mediterranean microclimate on Vancouver Island's beautiful Saanich Inlet.

Like Keats, **Gail M. Murray** seeks to capture the essence of the moment. Her writing is a response to her natural and emotional environment. Discover Gail's poems in *Written Tenfold, Blank Spaces, Wordscape, Arborealis,* and *The Banister.* Find her creative non-fiction in *The Globe and Mail, Devour, Trellis, Heartbeats, Renaissance, NOW Magazine, Blank Spaces,* and *Our Canada.*

Title: *Shame to Shine: The Wreckage & Rise From Domestic Violence*

Author: **Cher Obediah**

ISBN: 978-1-7782316-0-5

Number of Pages: 124

Published year: 2022

Reviewed by **Anna Nieminen**

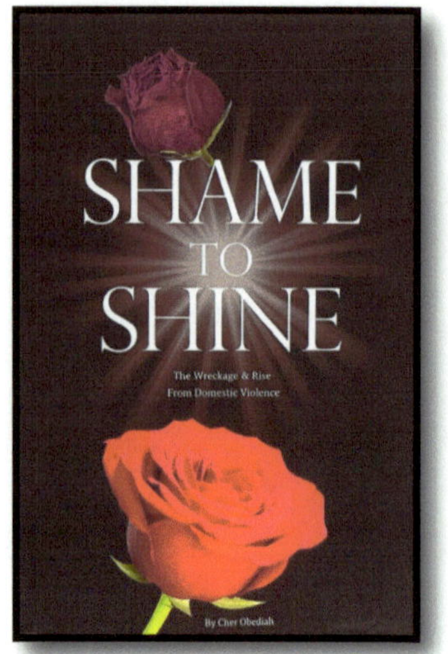

Shame to Shine: The Wreckage & Rise From Domestic Violence is the first poetry book by Cher Obediah, who describes it as "my voice unmuted, my diary exposed, snapshots of my experiences". The multi-talented Obediah includes 24 drawings to illustrate 60 poems on themes such as love, loss, trauma, verbal abuse, manipulation, healing, transformation, and empowerment.

Chapter I – The Cycle of Domestic Violence begins with "First Kiss" about anticipation, playful awkwardness, and memorizing special moments. The book quickly changes theme: the words "his temper" open "The Red Road" about supporting her partner's recovery as a survivor of colonialism and intergenerational trauma. An illustration of their feet in moccasins poking out from under a blanket evokes more empathy. In "Little White Lies", verbal assaults make it plain that her partner's past will continue to affect their present, but Obediah is in denial about her own historical trauma, believing she's "unaffected" as the daughter of urban Indigenous parents.

Chapter I includes two more romantic poems, "Our Island" and "Mornings Like This," while the remainder describe escalating abuse involving raised fists and spitting on the floor. "Coffee Chaos" recounts her distress about the "war on the windshield," yet another incident when Obediah's abuser "mangled my mind." There's a change with "Crazymaking." Obediah repeats the words "I'm sorry..." but is being ironic rather than apologetic, and she's "disgusted' and "repulsed." The chapter ends with "Final Image" about her partner's infidelity: "I feel foolish falling in love/ with a fool like him." The power of Obediah's poetry is in her willingness to be vividly vulnerable so that other survivors can feel validation and connection.

Chapter II – Healing and Transformation starts with two poems about loss and continues with poems describing Obediah engaging with various healing practices such as counselling, yoga, guidance from dreams about her brother in the spirit world, and Buddhism, while she remains entangled: "our energies circle ready for a round/ of relationship roulette." By the end of the chapter, Obediah is "Harvesting Peace."

Chapter III – Enlightenment and Empowerment contains poems about forgiveness, acceptance, trusting intuition, the healing power of "nature like a relative," and self-love. Obediah's restoration through connection with her Indigenous roots is particularly vivid in "Ode to the Elements": "I am a divine collage/ of all elements/ built to belong in balance/ I am a radiant miracle of creation." "The Trail", with its description of the "perpetual poetry" of the forest "beyond the borders of the birch," paired with an endearing drawing of Obediah walking with her dog, is likely to appeal to both survivors and a general audience. Indeed, many of the poems offer wisdom and guidance for finding self-worth and inner peace.

Shame to Shine is powerful truth-telling that engages the reader in learning about the psychological side of domestic violence, including how colonialism and generational trauma intersect with male privilege. Obediah inspires hope through describing multiple paths for restoration of lives and dreams, including the act of writing one's way back to the light and liberation.

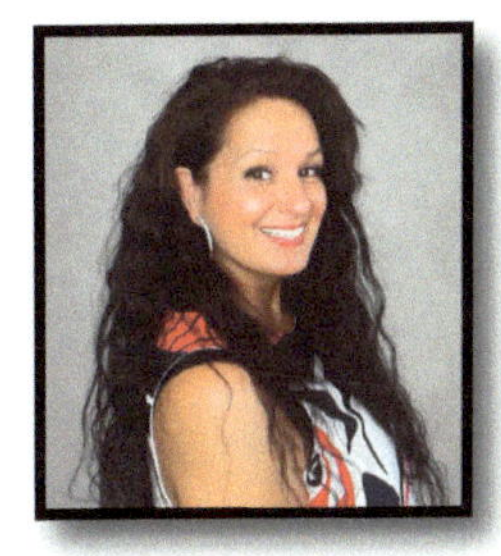

Cher Obediah is Ojibway and Mohawk of the Turtle Clan from Six Nations with roots in Alderville First Nation. She's a filmmaker, writer and speaker who focuses on projects that promote Indigenous culture, healing and transformation, social change, youth driven projects and content that inspires others to recognize their worth.

Anna Nieminen lives and works in Scarborough, Ontario, where she co-facilitates the Scarborough Poetry Club. She is a poetry curator. She guest curated a series of poetry events during Ontario Culture Days 2015 for Scarborough Arts and was the Literary Juror for their Big Art Book: En Route in 2016.

Title: *In Love With The Night*
Author: **Liz Torlée**
ISBN: 9781927882764
Number of Pages: 244
Published Year: 2022

Reviewed by: **Felicity Sidnell Reid**

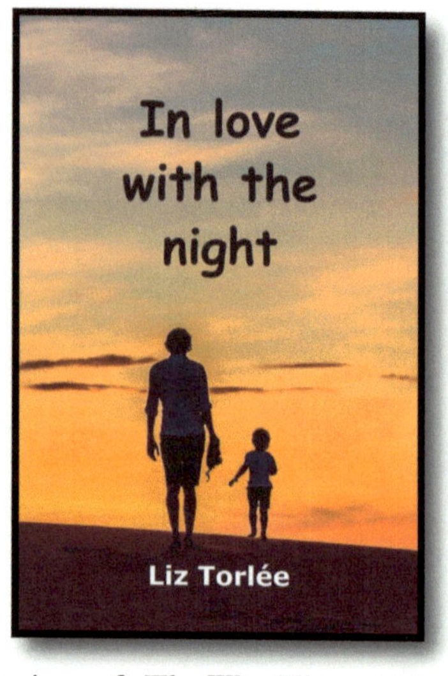

In Love With The Night, Torlée's second novel includes several characters from her first book, *The Way Things Fall*: antique dealers and partners from Toronto, Nigel and Philippe; the now successful painter Steven Farrow; and Lukas, the young son of the two central characters, Karl Gustav and Rachel Covelli. Several years after the conclusion of *The Way Things Fall*, these characters are brought together by the complicated relationships they had with the now dead Rachel and the fallout from her relationship with her Svengalian lover, astronomer, astrologist, and Egyptologist, Karl Gustav. Old secrets are disclosed as the beggar, Amina Gamel, learns of her beloved father's behavior after an incident brings her, as a valued and loved employee, into the family of Hadir and Dominic El Hassan, wealthy owners of a boutique hotel in Fez, Morocco and who are about to expand their business by opening a new hotel in Toronto.

Despite the connections, Torlée's two novels are very different in mood; the first story is frequently dark and ends tragically. *In Love With The Night* however is a bildungsroman, tracing Amina's maturation, her growing affection for the little boy Lukas, and the blossoming of her relationship with the man she has always loved.

Though questions of fate and coincidence underlie the plot of *In Love With The Night*—for example, bringing together Amina, the El Hassan family, the artist Steven Farrow, Nigel, and Lukas—Amina's challenges arise primarily from her search for the truth about her father, his actions and motivation, and her desire to behave in a moral and principled way. She has to come to terms with what she discovers and make difficult decisions when she becomes involved with a group of people who plan to defraud her of money her father left her when he died.

In Love With The Night's large cast of characters come alive as their relationships, like that between Amina and Sophie El Hassan, deepen. The El Hassans emerge as a close affectionate family dealing with inevitable family tensions in their individual ways. Steven Farrow's old friend Nigel's abiding love for Rachel and his anxiety about the future of her son pull him into the centre of the plot.

Torlée's skill at description enables her to conjure up the sights, sounds, tastes, and ambience of the story's locales, allowing the reader to travel with the characters to the Moroccan city of Fez and its bustling *souk,* into the El Hassan family hotel, across the desert to the pyramids of Egypt, as well as to Niagara Falls, and, through the eyes of Amina, to the city of Toronto in the summer.

The novel has engaging characters, a twisty plot, and plenty of secrets and surprises to keep a reader turning the pages.

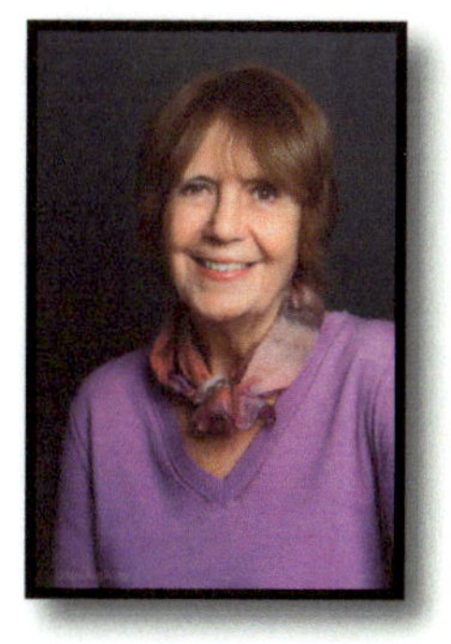

Liz Torlée lived and worked in England and Germany before emigrating to Canada. She has always been fascinated by the idea of fate and the way it makes all our lives intersect in strange and far-reaching ways. She and her husband are avid travellers, especially through the Middle East … or any country with a desert! They live in mid-town Toronto. *In Love with the Night* is Liz's second novel.

Felicity Sidnell Reid is the author of a book for teachers, a series of textbooks for language learners, a novel: *Alone: A Winter in the Woods* (Hidden Brook Press, 2015, e-book in 2020), and poetry collections: *The Yellow Magnolia* (Glentula Press, 2021) and *The Many Faces* (Aeolus House, 2022). She is the co-producer and co-host of the weekly literary radio series, *Word on the Hills*. She chaired two Spirit of the Hills Arts Festivals in 2017 and 2019 and is a director and secretary of the rebranded Northumberland Festival of the Arts.

Title: *The Last Secret*

Author: **Pam Royl**

ISBN: 9781927882733

Number of Pages: 224

Published Year: 2022

Reviewed by **Susan Statham**

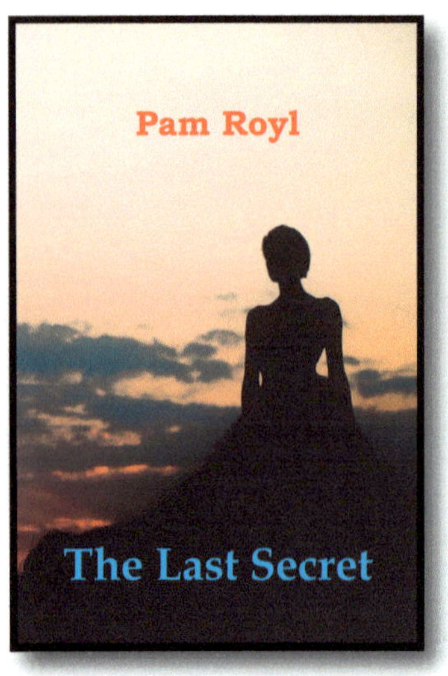

In *The Last Secret*, Pam Royl takes a proud and high-spirited young woman through a 19th century maze of deception. Sarah Denton claws at the secrets erected to both protect and imprison her. At the same time, she conceals much from those she loves. But nothing, it seems, can remain hidden forever.

Forced into purple silk and multiple crinolines, Sarah attends a gala commemorating the opening of Victoria Hall by His Royal Highness, The Prince of Wales. To her mother's dismay, it's not the well-heeled young men of this small Ontario town that interest her daughter. Sarah is instantly smitten by the bulging muscles and tumbling black curls of one Joseph Drury — a man, she says, "whose Scottish lilt curls around my heart."

In England, Sarah's father had been a village blacksmith, but in this "crude colony" he transforms himself into the owner of a thriving iron foundry. This rise in status prompts Sarah's mother to make decisions based solely on appearance. And while the older daughter, Tabitha, is compliant, Sarah doesn't want the gilded cage. She may "only be a woman," but it's independence that she's after. Her attraction to Joe Drury deepens when he takes her to view his family's land.

Sarah soon discovers that those who profess love, wrap it in many conditions. By defying her mother's rules, she is essentially disowned. And though he's there for her in time of need, her father's generosity is quickly withdrawn. Tabitha too takes an undeserved prize she would not have received had she been honest about her situation. Happy with a husband who provides the channel to her ambition to own a dairy farm, Sarah discovers, too late, that he is also a pathway to destruction.

Throughout the ups and downs of *The Last Secret*, author Pam Royl's descriptive powers enliven her characters and capture the struggles of life in the 1870s:

Wiping sweat off my forehead with the sleeve of my filthy dress, I dug out another pitchfork of straw and shook it over the rotting, smelly floor.

That night the winter bore down heavily upon us, with snow driving against the cottage, mounding up around its windows, swallowing us into its frozen jowls.

Although secrets are the engine of this novel, there are moments near the end of the book when the protagonist echoes the feelings of the reader: *I was tired of secrets.* At 212 pages, however, the reader is not made to wait too long for revelation and resolution. Based on a true story, *The Last Secret* is a novel the real Sarah Denton would be proud to call her own.

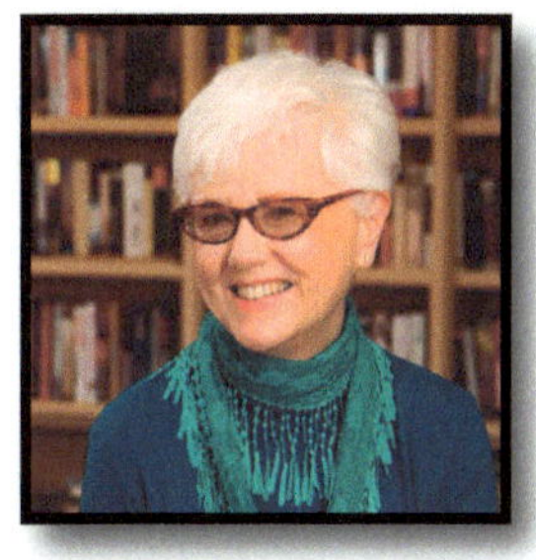

Pam Royl was inspired to write her debut novel by an ancestor she discovered while writing family memoirs. Developing her fiction writing skills through courses at the University of Toronto, and under the mentorship of International award-winning author, Donna Morrissey, Pam set her story within the fascinating history of Northumberland County, where she lives with her husband, Ian.

Susan Statham is an author and a visual artist. She is the editor and contributor for *Hill Spirits V* and co-editor and contributor for all previous *Hill Spirits* anthologies. *The Painter's Craft,* her first mystery novel, features artist and amateur detective, Maud Gibbons. Her second novel, *True Image,* is under review and her third, *Caged,* is in progress.

Title: *Thorneside Stories – A Mix of Sun and Cloud*

Author: **Christopher Cameron.**

ISBN: 9781771805568

Number of Pages: 280

Published Year: 2022

Reviewed by **Shane Joseph**

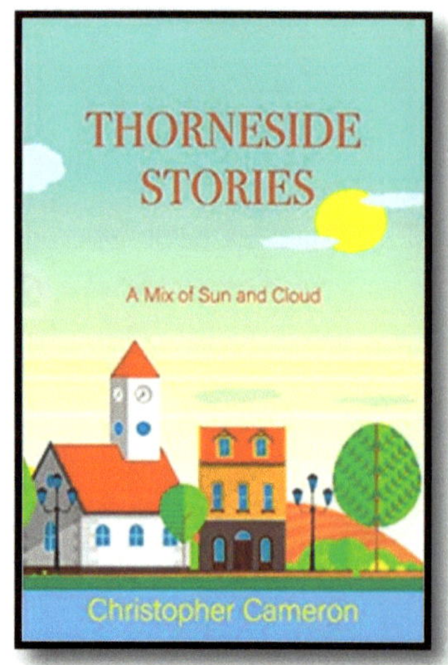

A sensitively and humorously rendered set of sketches of small-town life during a whole year beginning in Autumn and ending the following Summer.

With his acute perception of the feminine viewpoint, I wondered why Christopher Cameron had not decided to turn this loose collection into a more satisfying novel by trimming down the number of extraneous members (and their digressive stories) of St. Ninian's choir and focusing instead on his four principals of the Women's Bridge Club to reveal them even more than he did by having them merely skinny dip (Commando, as they prefer to call it) and bond on a rock in the middle of a deserted lake?

However, as he chose to go in order of season, include the whole town, and begin with a cast of largely forgettable choristers, we meander through glib, safe Protestant life of retiring Archdeacons rendering farewell stump speeches and church cannons with pesky flycatchers, until we get to the four women, and then the book takes off. Lurking behind the safe façade of middle-class respectability and the religious and social rituals of small-town life is a desire for more, a desire to cheat on the side, a desire to be authentic, and these desires lead to all sorts of complicated, tragic, and hilarious situations. Humour, pithy observations, and eloquent writing drip off every page, making this an easy and pleasurable read, despite us wondering where the author is going to wander off next.

Two other characters of interest are church organist Ashley who nurses a secret life, and jogger Chuck, although I wondered how the latter could reconcile his physical fitness regimen with his fondness for alcohol—

something had to give, sooner or later—instead, he attracts a lover! And of course, the mysterious Lucas Darnell helps tie up many of the loose story strands floating around Thorneside. As I also live in the area from which the author draws his inspiration, I got a kick out of trying to match the names of the fictional places— i.e., Thorneside, Lockport, Port Percy, Workforth and Hoostens, not forgetting Lindisfarne County—with their real-life equivalents. I agree, given the salacious matter lying beneath the "respectable" lives of these church-going WASPs, it was wise of Cameron to fictionalize the setting.

There are at least half a dozen novels here – each of the principal characters could easily deliver one—and I believe Cameron is teasing us with an "executive summary" of small-town life through this collection. I hope he sits down (soon) to take each one of these characters apart and render those follow-up novels in greater depth. For a big city guy who retired to a small town not-so long ago, he has a remarkable eye for the "types" that rural communities generate.

In his acknowledgements section, the author quotes Galbraith and admits that he (Cameron) "talks too much." I have to agree. "Brevity is the soul of wit," would apply here, and if some excessive descriptions, some unnecessary chapters, and a whole raft of peripheral characters had been eliminated, this would have amounted to a taut novel or linked story collection while retaining the author's signature humour.

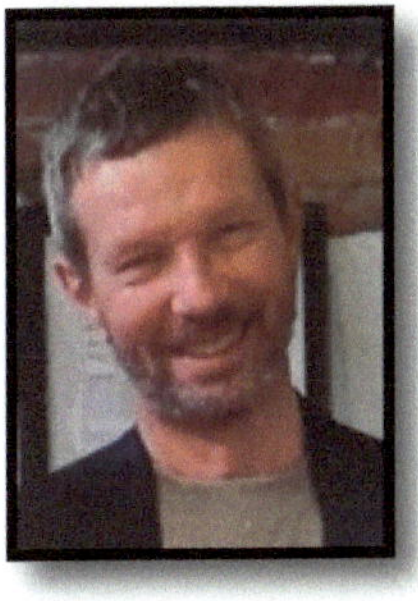

Christopher Cameron enjoyed a long and successful career as a professional opera singer, performing on stages across Canada and abroad and retiring in 2009. His lively memoir of those years, *Dr. Bartolo's Umbrella*, was published in 2017. Now, as writer, magazine editor, and co-host of a local radio show about writers, he spends his days immersed in stories of the people, places, and happenings in Northumberland County, Ontario. *Thorneside Stories* is his first book of fiction.

Shane Joseph is a Canadian novelist, blogger, reviewer, short story writer, and publisher. He is the author of seven novels and three collections of short stories. His latest novel, *Empire in the Sand*, was released in the Fall of 2022. For details visit his website at www.shanejoseph.com.

Title: ***The Many Faces***

Author: **Felicity Sidnell Reid**

ISBN: 9781987872453

Number of Pages: 94

Published Year: 2022

Reviewed by **Antony Di Nardo**

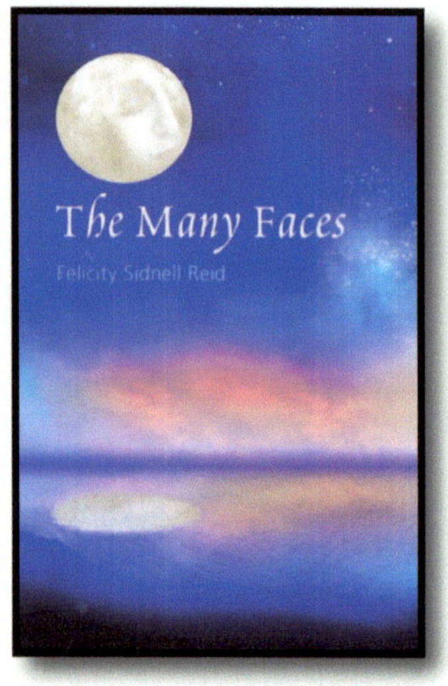

"My mother," writes Felicity Sidnell Reid, "tamped the radio / to a whisper … / her ear resting on the woven panel / of the radio, perched on the bookcase like a pigeon, / bringing her the world." Those lines, like many of the poems in *The Many Faces*, evoke a distant, yet familiar time and place, where the quotidian facts of life reveal themselves in simple gestures, essential moments. Listening is important to this poet, listening and connecting to the world. For her, the act of listening is effectively translated into narratives and imagery that record the passing of time and tell of how, with the right words, time can anchor memories that render life meaningful and relevant. In this poet's hands, language lives up to its claim that experience can not only be described but enriched by the very language that speaks it.

Description is the art of compression and, in these poems, an entire universe of feelings, memories and heartfelt observations, someone's life complete, has been compressed into a nutshell. The poems are forged in narratives that tell stories framed by anecdotes, details and rubrics of an age that gave us the present. And in this present time, we hear the voice of a poet that re-enacts the past with imagery polished to a patina that's tangible and accessible.

Seamus Heaney and W.H. Auden are present in this book, the ghosts of both these poets hovering over many of the lines. In her poem "Limbo," Heaney actually makes a cameo appearance. We're told that "When Seamus Heaney came to lunch … I cooked him fish" and then the speaker proceeds to tell the mournful tale of a still birth. There is controlled pathos in these lines, the kind of control one expects to find in every line this poet writes.

One of the strongest pieces in this collection is "The Lookout," a sweeping lyric that embraces nature's resilience despite our menacing footprint on a planet now redolent with "issues of the Anthropocene that stiffen our tongue / thicken our speech." Sidnell Reid cautions the reader on the fragility of our Earth. Her language is so robust and engaged that it seems to defy our own ignorance when it comes to the impact we are having as *homo-industrialist*. The poem concludes with this gorgeous, yet ironic, line: "And, for now, the skies over Beijing blossom blue."

Felicity Sidnell Reid has given us something to think about in *The Many Faces*. Her poems compress time and place into compact narratives that rejoice in the precision of language, poems that revel in descriptions of both the past and present. If Sidnell Reid were a painter, trading the imagery of language for a set of brushes, many of these poems would be watercolours: delicate, yet precise; bold and bright, but always sensitive to light and shadow. And suitable for framing.

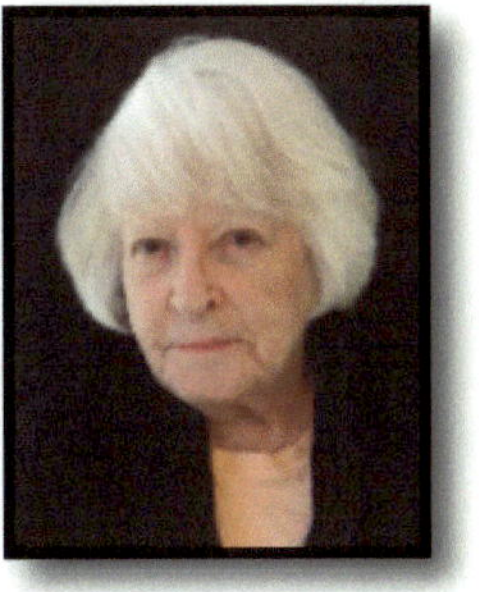

Felicity Sidnell Reid is the author of a book for teachers, a series of textbooks for language learners, a novel: *Alone: A Winter in the Woods* (Hidden Brook Press, 2015, e-book in 2020), and poetry collections: *The Yellow Magnolia* (Glentula Press, 2021) and *The Many Faces* (Aeolus House, 2022). She is the co-producer and co-host of the weekly literary radio series, *Word on the Hills*. She chaired two Spirit of the Hills Arts Festivals in 2017 and 2019 and is a director and secretary of the rebranded Northumberland Festival of the Arts.

Antony Di Nardo is an award-winning poet and editor. His latest collection, *Forget-Sadness-Grass* (Ronsdale Press), was a CBC Books' poetry pick for Fall 2022. His previous book, *Through Yonder Window Breaks*, won the inaugural Don Gutteridge Poetry Award. His work has been translated into several languages and appears widely in journals and anthologies. He divides his time between Sutton, Quebec and Cobourg, Ontario.

F r a g m e n t i s m
the new movement in literature?

by Shane Joseph

Every fifty years or so, a new movement overcomes art, in particular literature. Thus, over the last two hundred years, we had Romanticism, Realism (and its offshoot Naturalism), Modernism and Post-Modernism that took us to the turn of the 21st century. The current movement, born in the present century, will take some time to be labelled; the pundits typically will wrestle and argue over it until its fifty-year lifespan is nearly exhausted before settling on a compromise nomenclature. For now, it veers between several names: trans-post modernism, post-millennialism, post-truth, pseudo-modernism, digi-modernism, meta-modernism and the very dull post-post-modernism.

Movements give birth to forms of expression. The general forms of literature, which I call the Big Four—i.e., non-fiction, fiction, poetry and drama—have stayed more or less the same over the last two centuries while the genres within them have evolved. So, within those general forms we've had stream-of-consciousness novels, free-verse poetry, autobiographical-fiction, creative-non-fiction, literary fiction, fan-fiction and a myriad of others. In fact, a writer's claim to fame has been to invent the next "big idea" – like Joyce, Sebald, and Proust did and succeeded, while a host of wannabes tried and failed. Some new genres have come and stayed; others have died out or morphed into hybrids.

Drilling down to another level, forms give birth and purpose to channels, or media, through which they are delivered to audiences. Conversely, forms also get exponential bursts whenever channel inventions come along: Gutenberg's press, radio, film and television being some of these channel inventions. And now with internet technology and the explosion of DIY tech tools, the 21st century is turbo charged with channel proliferation. Therefore, while the pundits argue about what the new literary movement of the first half of the 21st century is going to be named, I'd like to call it **Fragmentism**, where the order of evolution has been reversed, *where Technology drives Channel which is driving Form and thus is ultimately driving evolution of the new Movement.* An unforeseen affirmation of McLuhan's "the Medium is the Message." I'd extend that to "the Medium is the Movement."

So, what's different in this millennium (it's actually twenty-two years old and, had it been a human, should have received the keys to the house by now)? The internet and DIY technology has spawned multi-channels such as You Tube, Tik Tok, Social Media, streaming video, and websites that have in turn generated new forms such as the blog, the vlog, home-made books, amateur video and audio, podcasts, webcasts, photoshopped-art, e-books, social media posts, tweets and the five-second commercial – new forms of expression of varying length and duration, usually shorter and more direct than the traditional Big Four, that either extend traditional literary forms or threaten to usurp them. In short: the list of literary forms just got a lot longer in the 21st century, so let's not limit it to the Big Four anymore. Distribution of these newer forms is global at little or no cost, with the press of a button. They have broader popular appeal, for they are built around modern lifestyles and attention spans. Today's general reader would rather flick through a "stream of newsfeed" than through a confusing "stream of consciousness" in a novel.

The self-help tools for creating content have also improved, democratizing the creative process for those willing to embrace new technology. I chuckle when I think of how, in just the second half of the last century, a celebrity writer like John Le Carré used to handwrite his many drafts, have a secretary type them out, then scribble his modifications on to the typescript, have a copy editor decipher the entire mess, and require a whole production team to produce his novel. Today, authors could do it all themselves using a laptop (i.e., write, edit, typeset, and design) and upload their novel to an online platform like Amazon, sans the cache that Le Carré built for himself for being a product of an age when the book was still a mysterious thing belonging to an elite aristocracy. Despite this freedom of creation, the modern writer has to navigate the many echo chambers of a diverse channel universe, and is forced to shout out their book from virtual rooftops to build a brand for the next several months until they and their book are ultimately "drowned in the feed," whereas Le Carré usually went on holiday after submitting his next book and had nothing more to do with it, and his work continued to reign on the bestseller shelf long after he died.

There is even a new generation of DIY tech tools approaching prime time, wherein the author will upload the desired characters and their descriptions, plot points, setting, genre, and let a book-writing application churn out a novel or story based on algorithms that have mapped out the structure of those literary genres. Thus, while the author is able to consolidate the means of production and distribution on a laptop, unlike poor Mr. Le Carré, the process of creation is fragmented between the author and this host of technological tools, while distribution is fragmented along a plethora of new channels. Who can claim true ownership for the success of a composite or fragmented work like this? Human, machine, or a host of mechanized bots from whom we can purchase "likes" to create an imaginary halo of popularity? How much of this work can subsequently be plagiarized and re-formulated into other works by other creators claiming ownership? Should we finally give up on the proprietorship of ideas and the laws of copyright in this new age?

What does a creator do in this movement of Fragmentism? Abdicate to the machine completely, or use the technology to personal advantage in a composite effort at creation? Or retire? There is no going back from these technological breakthroughs – ask Gutenberg or Edison or Zuckerberg. It is hard to imagine a world now without the printing press, the movie, or social media, and soon, the metaverse. The key lies in accepting our present reality and re-defining what success means (do not use money, it might be depressing), learning to use the new tools, and engaging in this new arena that is a darned sight more multifarious and interesting than the old one that was overly compartmentalized and specialized.

Distilling it down to the art form I am most interested in, literature, what would writers look like in this time of Fragmentism? They too will be fragmented, being forced but enabled to multi-task, being multi-skilled in writing, editing, designing, producing audio and video, performing their work, and shamelessly promoting themselves. They will be jacks-of-all-trades and masters of some (or none). Financial rewards will come from unknown sources like advertising, crowd-funding, sponsorship, endorsement, the novelty lottery that commercial interests dip into periodically, and a second job (or a wealthy spouse or inheritance) – some of these reward sources existed during other movements, while some are entirely new. And all creators, including writers, are now able to connect directly with their audiences, instead of through a host of intermediaries – a fringe benefit, frightening to the introverts, liberating to the show-offs.

I know of many writers, especially those called "indies" (independently published or published by small presses) who dabble in some or all of these tasks. Some of these authors need help in aspects of video production, interviews, or social media promotion as it is hard to be a jack-of-all-trades overnight, just because the landscape changed. As a small publisher, I have assisted my authors where time and resources have permitted, while learning these skills on the fly myself. As for the brand name authors in the big houses, they too dabble in this multi-tasking, but have marketing and publicity departments to play these roles, so that they can do what they do best – write, and perform their work in front of pre-assembled audiences.

Welcome to the Age of Fragmentism – are you game to play, while the pundits grapple with trying to give this new movement a label?

Not to be confused with the Italian literary movement by the same name that began just before the First World War, characterised by the use of short pieces of dramatic prose and fragmentary images.

Author Bio

Shane Joseph is a Canadian novelist, blogger, reviewer, short story writer, editor, designer, video maker, promoter, and publisher. He is the author of seven novels and three collections of short stories. His latest novel, *Empire in the Sand*, was released in the Fall of 2022.

For details of Shane's multi-tasking, visit:
- His **author website** at www.shanejoseph.com
- His **publisher website** at Blue Denim Press: Focused on novels, short stories and selective non-fiction.
- His **Book Reviews**: Book Reviews – Shane Joseph
- His Writing on **Wattpad**: shanejoseph - Wattpad
- His **Blog**: Blog – Shane Joseph
- **Facebook** at Shane Joseph | Facebook
- **Twitter** at (4) Shane Joseph (@writershane) / Twitter
- **You Tube** at (239) Shane Joseph - YouTube
- **Instagram** at Shane Joseph (@shanewriterjoseph) • Instagram photos and videos
- **Goodreads** at Shane Joseph (Author of Redemption in Paradise) | Goodreads

He hasn't taken the plunge into Tik Tok yet, but is considering it.

Canada Coast to Coast to Coast

Photography Curator
Olaf Dijkstra

Last year Editor-in-chief, Richard / Tai asked me to become the photography curator for Devour: Art & Lit. I was very honoured. It inspired me to search for specific themes and to connect with other photographers.

One of them is Matt Shannon from Vancouver Island. He is a top-notch photographer, so we're very proud to introduce him as our feature photographer in this Winter issue, 015.

The theme for this issue is 'water'. From coast to coast to coast, Canada is surrounded by water, no matter how big this country is. Water could be streams, rivers, oceans, or lakes; all are plentiful and beautiful in Canada.

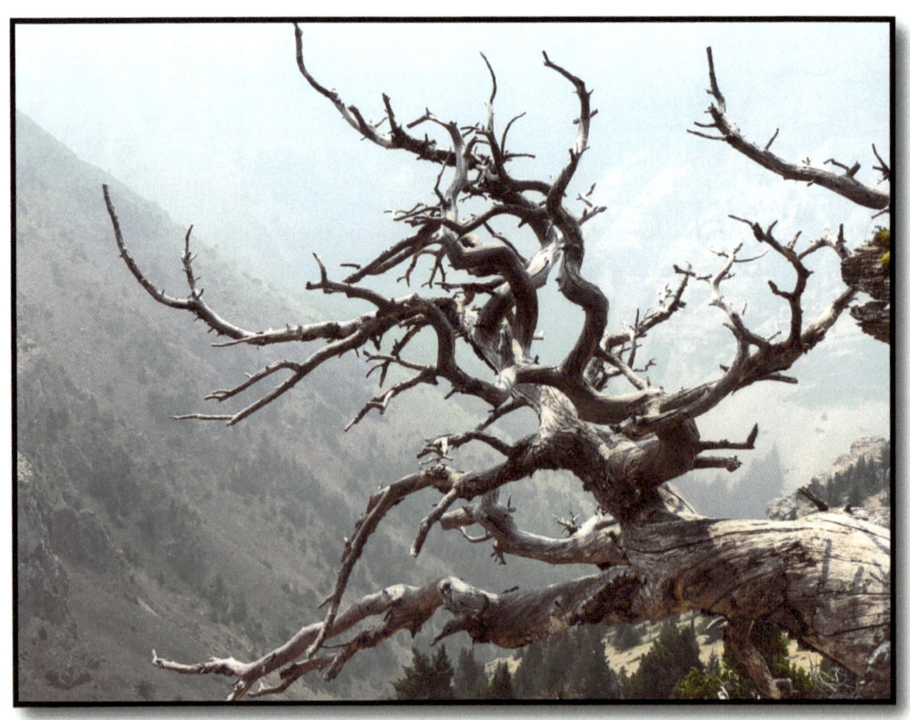

Branches getting air – Olaf Dijkstra

Olaf Dijkstra lives in West Kelowna, BC. He is originally from the Netherlands, but since 2011 a Permanent Resident of Canada. In 2000, he visited Canada for the first time. He said it was love at first sight. Six years later he started his application process and moved with his family in 2011. "You can say it was a 'calling of the wild' for me. Lots of space, nature, wildlife and ideal for me as I like to travel and take photos while travelling." Every spring/summer he guides Dutch tourists through the province on a few trips.

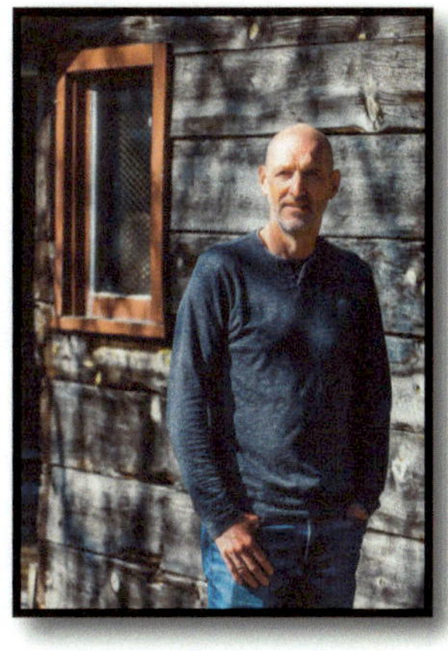

During covid, travelling was hard, so instead he decided to visit ghost towns in British Columbia. This eventually led to the creation of his website https://olafincanada.ca/, where you can enjoy his photos about landscapes, wildlife and abandoned places in BC and Alberta.

See his "Abandoned in BC" photographs in the past issue #013 at: www.issuu.com/richardgrove1

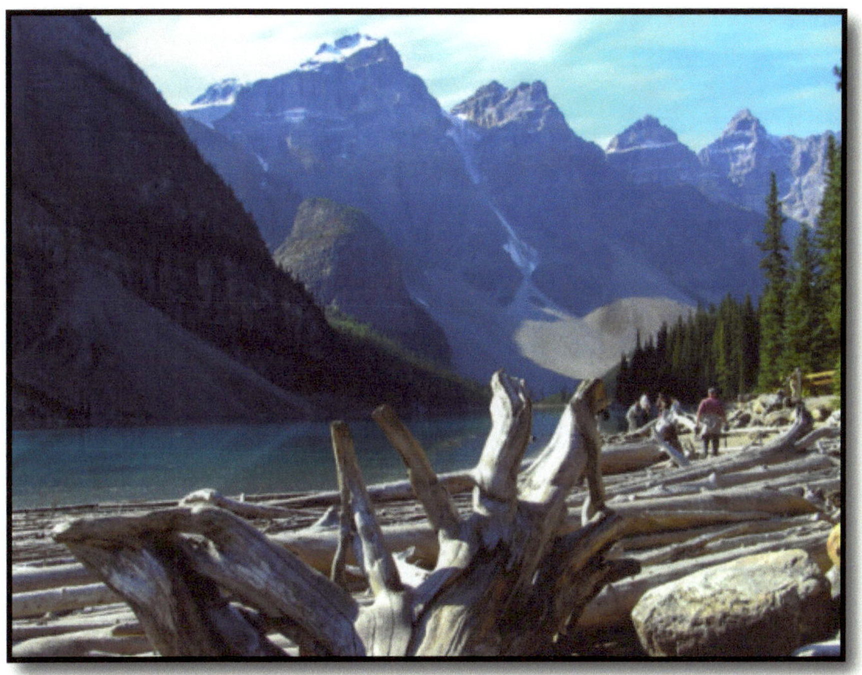

Moraine Lake – Olaf Dijkstra

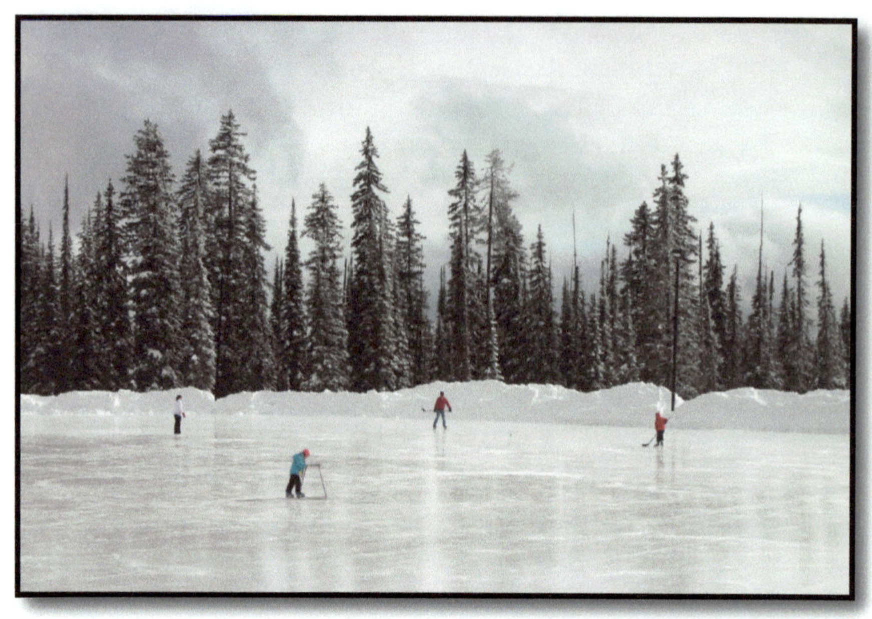

Hockey at Big White – Olaf Dijkstra

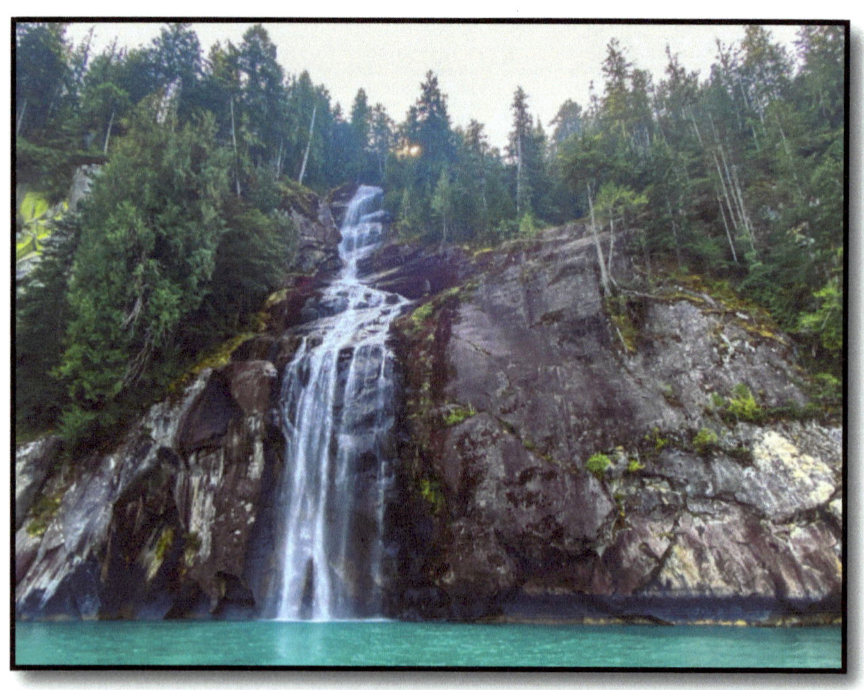

Waterfall near Campbell River – Olaf Dijkstra

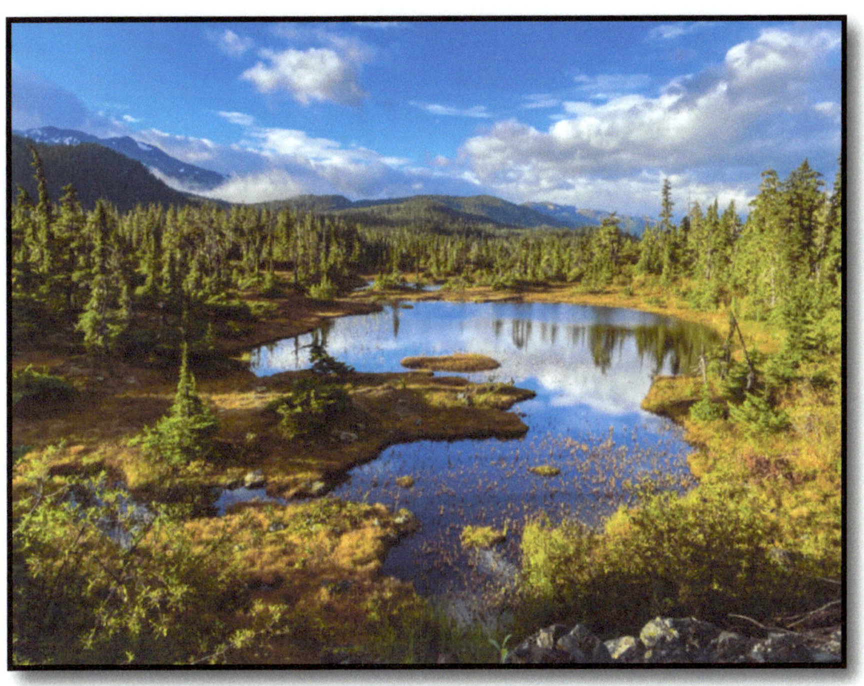

Lake near Kitsault – Olaf Dijkstra

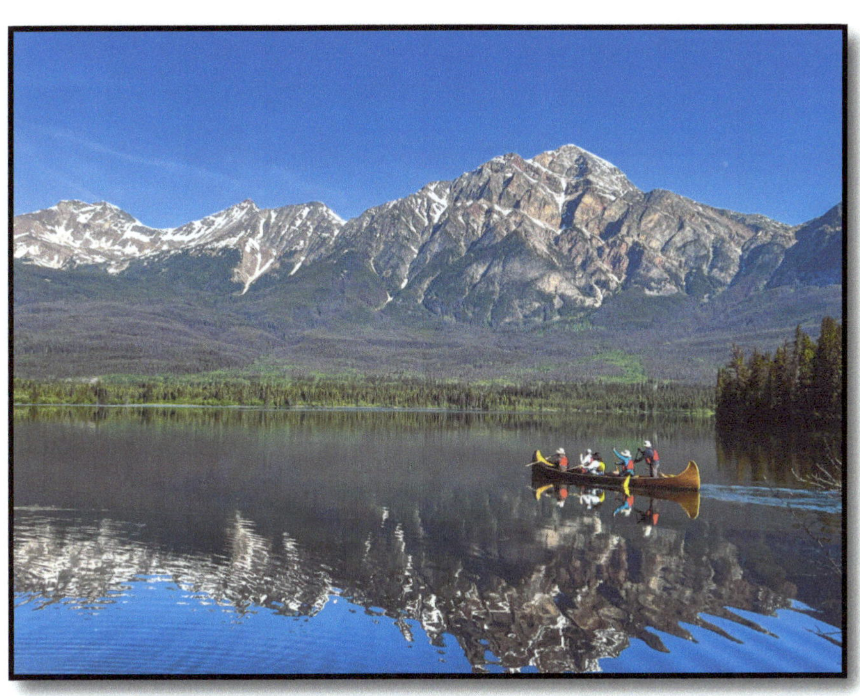

Patricia Lake – Olaf Dijkstra

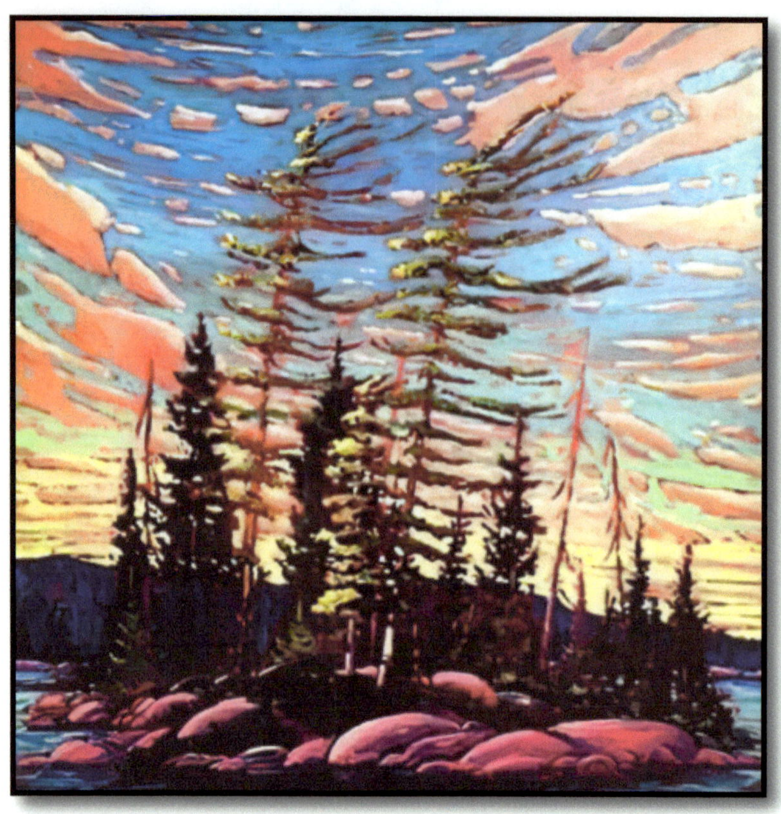

Algonquin Evening, Acrylic, 30x30, Andrew Hamilton

An Interview with
Andrew Hamilton

By Kimberley E. Grove

Entrepreneur: *a person who <u>organizes</u> and operates a business or businesses, taking on greater than normal financial risks in order to do so.*

Even though the definition of an entrepreneur includes taking financial risk, Andrew Hamilton is an entrepreneur in an even more creative mode. He will start a business, not because he wants to make vast quantities of money but because he has an idea that he wants to pursue. He tried the traditional career path when his father encouraged him to get a job and he became a nurse. But he soon found it unfulfilling because it was too predictable. It was so routine that it became boring. He saw creativity as more attractive. "The most challenging thing was seeing what was inside myself." So he decided to make a change.

Andrew left nursing to become an artist. At 16 he had bicycled around the Gaspe area and at one point when seeing a picturesque sight of a small town on a hill, he imagined a painting in his mind. He has realized that he had been doing that most of his life. Whereas some might imagine a photograph from something they see, Andrew saw a scene that he wanted to pursue as a painting. So at 30, even though he had failed art in high school twice, he decided to apply to the Ontario College of Art after putting together a sketchbook. He had always enjoyed drawing, but he hadn't realized what a passion it was in his life until he followed his dream. He was accepted at OCA but pigeonholed into the illustration and design program where he would get training that would lead to a career. However he saw the whole career thing as society's limitation in life. He

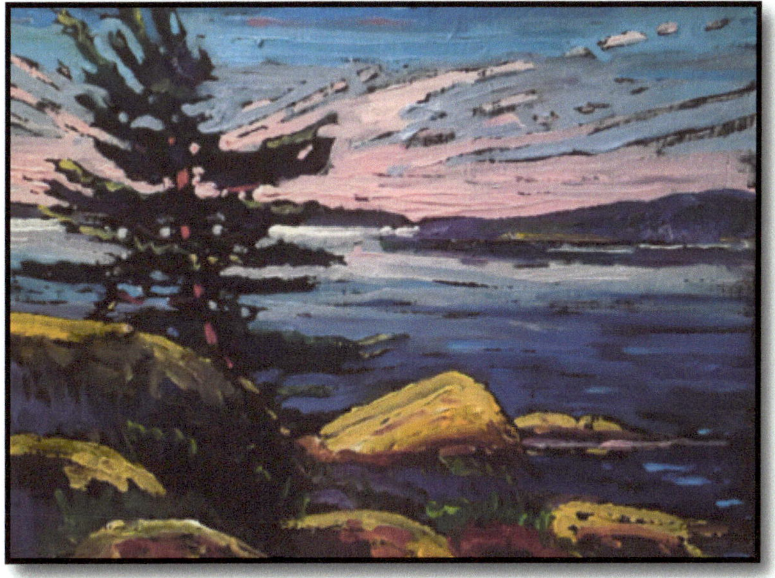

Georgian Bay Sunset, Oil, 6x8, Andrew Hamilton

had already had a health care business and a gardening business but he sold them both. He had bought and sold houses that he renovated. "I turned my back on that. I could always go back. I have so many things that fascinate and interest me," he said. He was ready for a new challenge. He views success as doing what one has a passion for. "I never want to be Hollywood successful." "So after Andrew told the art teachers he was there to learn to draw and paint, he

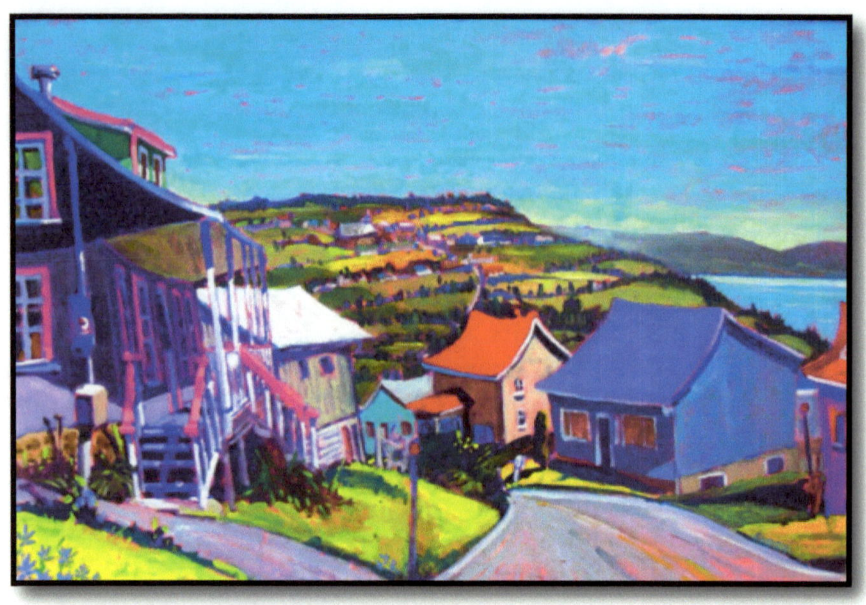

Road to Charlevoix, Acrylic, 30x40, Andrew Hamilton

transferred into an inter-disciplinary program where he was able to do print making and painting as his major and minor studies. He also took pottery and sculpting. "It's not about the money. It's about what I would like to explore." He is quite the inspiration for any young person wondering what to do with their life. And so began his artist adventure. At OCA it was the teachers that were out of the ordinary that really impressed him. They were like minded to him in that they tended to give exercises that were out of the ordinary. One such teacher, Victor Tinkl, had the students bring a wooden chair to class and the assignment was to take it apart and then make art out of it. One student put it in a chipper and used the chippings to make a sculpture. It was the creative thinking outside the box that he loved. Following this type of thinking it occurred to him that he could do a painting a day. So one year he did just that. The 365 oil paintings were 6 x 8 but each was different, teaching him more about his craft, about colour, about paint about inspiration. Eventually, his creations were noticed. He was asked to teach at St Lawrence School of Fine arts in Brockville. He became a professor and has never stopped teaching, but no longer in an institution. One of the things he had learned at OCA was what makes a good teacher and what makes a poor teacher. He had witnessed some fine teachers there. He remembered in high school an art teacher insisting that the class draw circles, triangles and squares. But he wanted to draw an old century home. If she had been a good teacher she would have seen the circles, triangles and

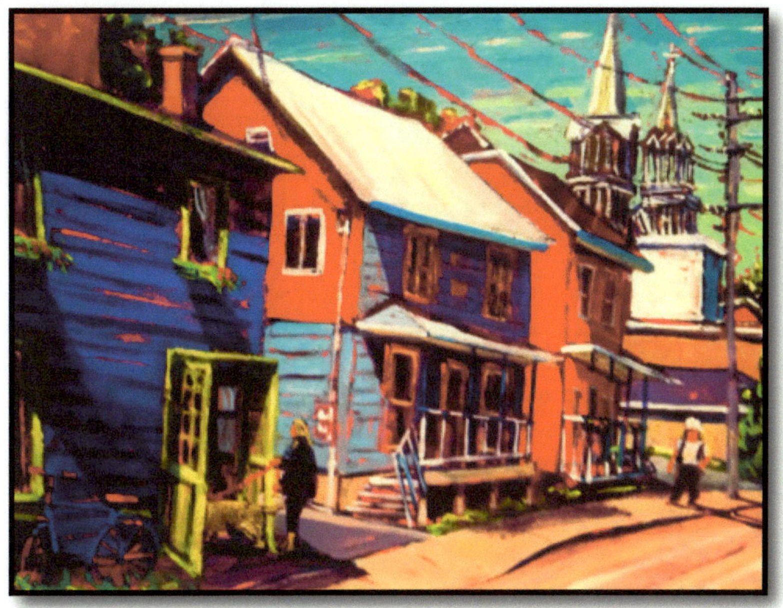

Le Shopping, Acrylic, 12x16, Andrew Hamilton

squares in the old home and encouraged a painting. Instead, she complained that he wasn't following the assignment.

Andrew lives a life that is out of the ordinary. After nursing his parents before they died and losing an uncle close to the same time, he decided to reassess his life again. For him, reinventing one's life is a constant process. "I retired at 39 in my head. I didn't want to wait until I was 65 until I would become an artist." He finds the artist's life to be rewarding. Every day is

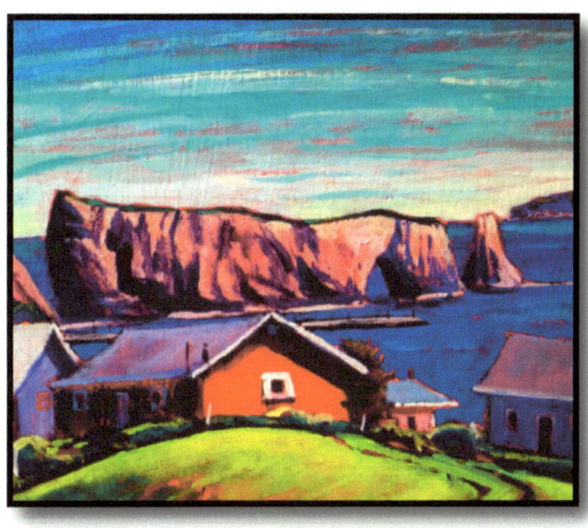

Gasping at the Gaspe,
Acrylic, 9x12,
Andrew Hamilton

mine. I don't feel like I'm working. I have chosen how to spend my time. It is never the same because I just listen to my gut and decide to do something." He sees time as one of the most valuable aspects of life. Someone once told him that he never sticks to anything. "I'm never stuck," was his response. "I'm growing and that is what I'm choosing. I have never felt stagnant."

Currently, his list of things he would like to do is about 100. He has a driveway full of driftwood that he collected for sculptures. Where others see garbage or recycle material, he sees art objects. He has a saying. "One object for the world and one for me." Andrew isn't afraid to put a sculpture that might be classified as "different" in front of his house. Afterall, he wants to share his creative spirit with those around him.

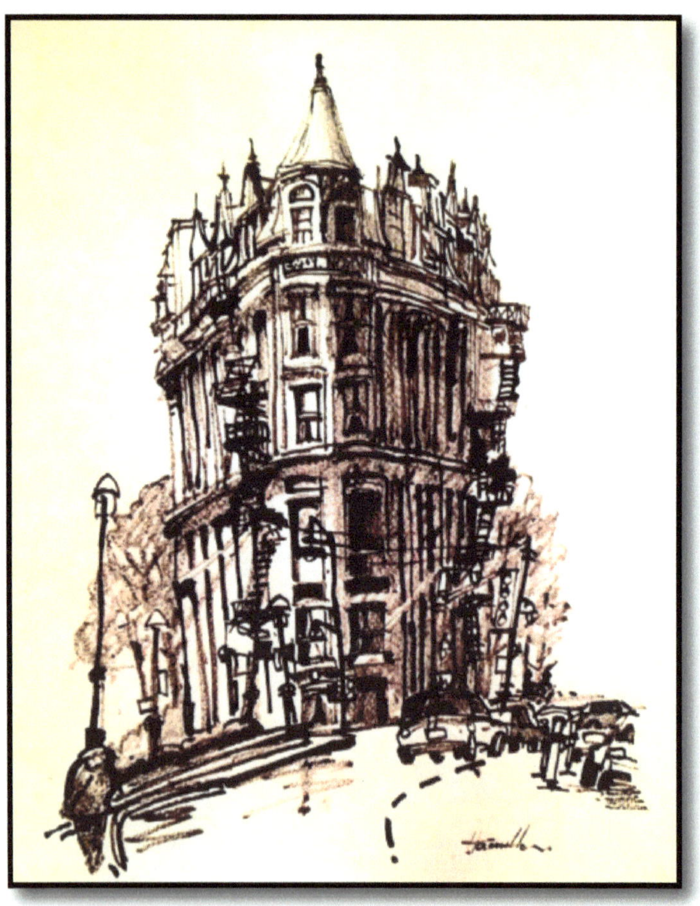

Flatiron Building, Ink drawn with twig, 9x12, Andrew Hamilton

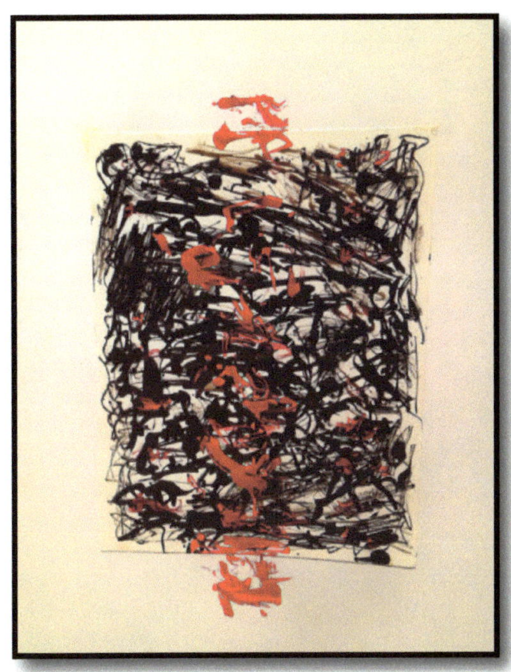

Cold Mountain series,
Ink and acrylic, 6x8
Andrew Hamilton

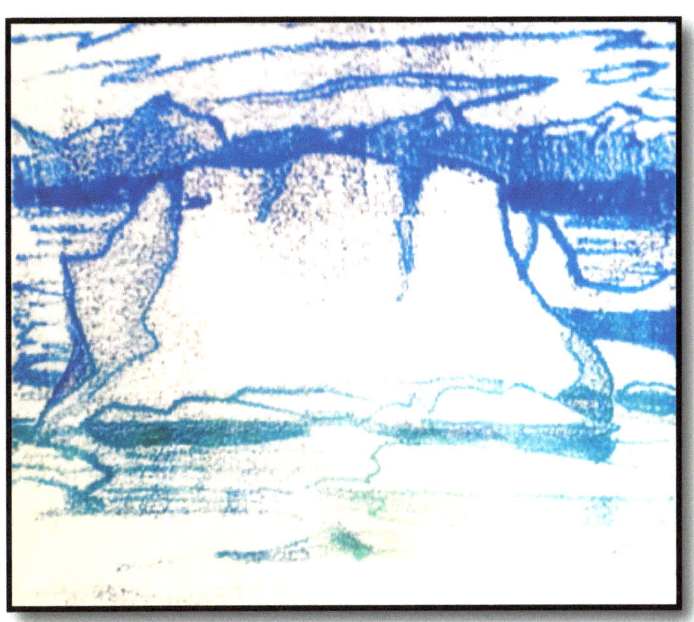

Iceberg Alley, Acrylic Monoprint, 6x8, Andrew Hamilton

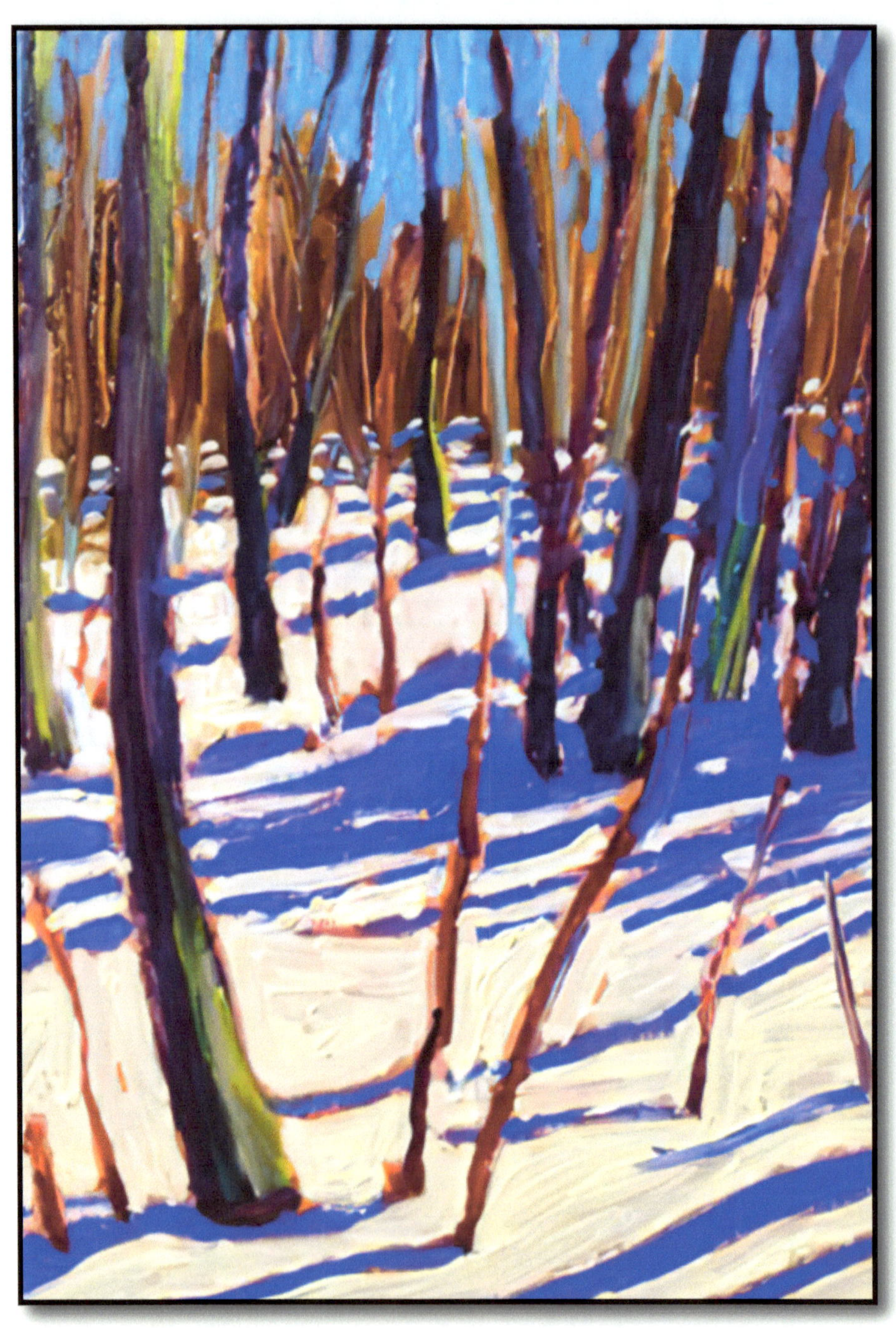

Afternoon hillside, Oil, 6x8, Andrew Hamilton

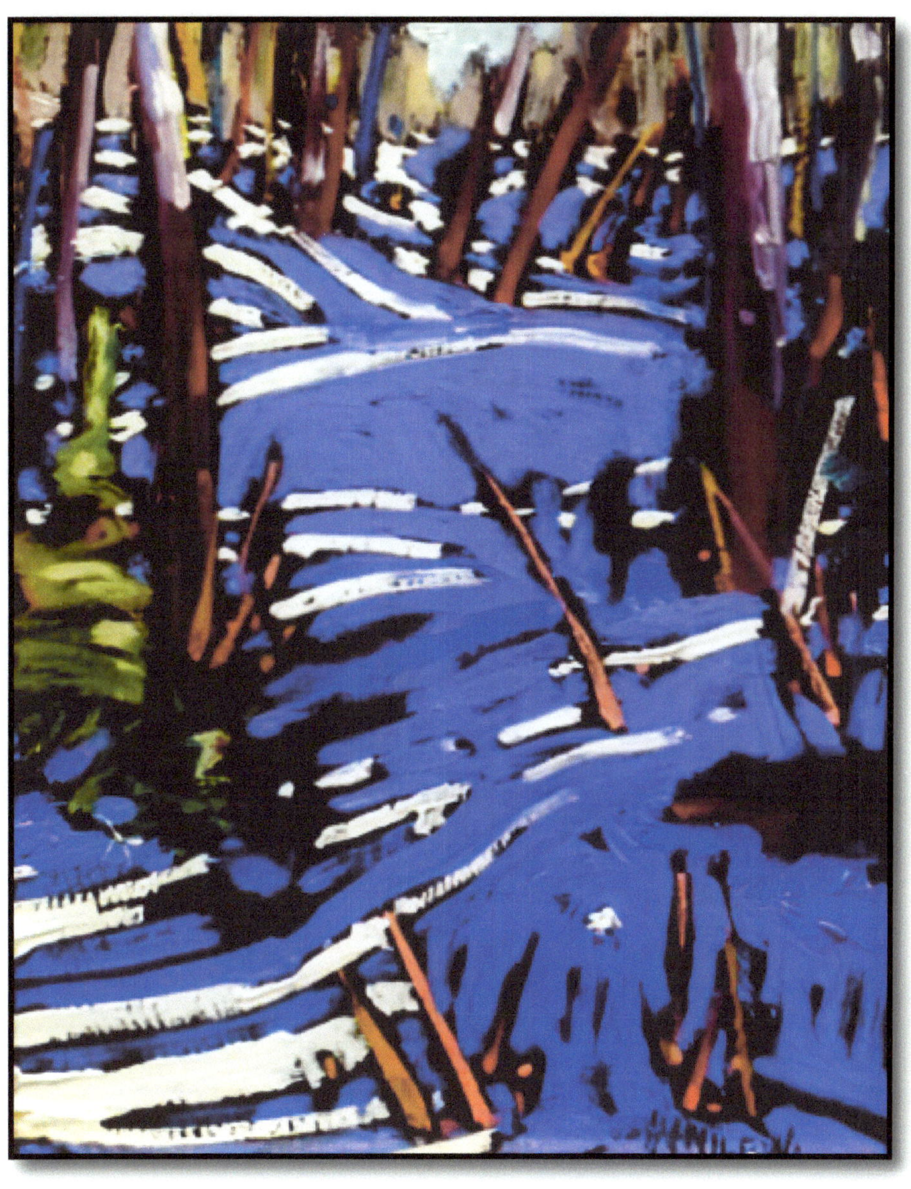

Snow Shadows, Oil, 6x8, Andrew Hamilton

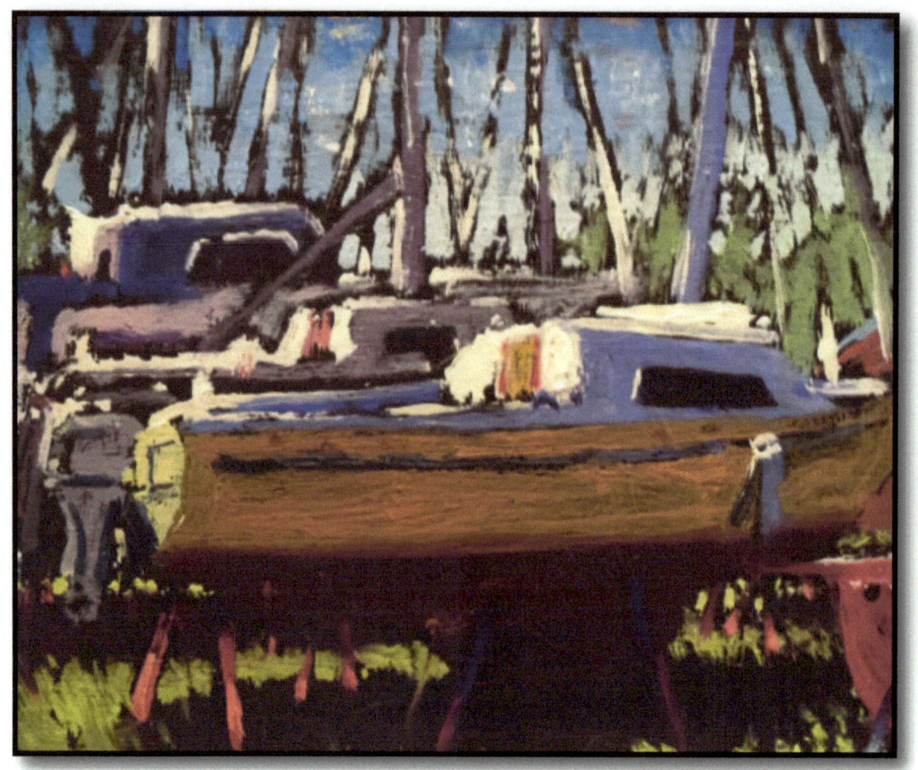

Sailing Dreams, Oil, 6x8, Andrew Hamilton

He has been reminded of Victor Tinkl's comment, "Make your life an art piece." He bought a house to make it a home and an art gallery. It was a haven where he could continue making art while displaying his passion to visitors. His gallery is open on the weekends at 96 Main Street, Brighton, Ontario. Be prepared to be awed.

Andrew Hamilton is a **Canadian Drawing Master**, a **Professor of Fine Arts** and is an accomplished, award winning painter in acrylic, oil and watercolor mediums. Using a highly imaginative palette of the three primaries plus white he has learned that all the colors of the universe are at hand. Combining this with a loose, inventive colorful style and with great freshness and immediacy he paints the landscape. Painting mostly on location, En Plein Air, Andrew paints in all four seasons capturing the beauty and natural rhythms of each. Andrew has painted from coast to coast traveling painting and capturing in paint this vast land. Using various media and traveling extensively, Andrew captures the rhythms, colors and moods of the landscape that inspires him.

Andrew studied in Victoria and four years at OCAD. In his last year at OCAD Andrew had the privilege of apprenticing with acclaimed Canadian landscape painter Doris McCarthy for a year and a half who for many years studied and worked with the famed Canadian Group of Seven. Andrew is inspired to follow in their landscape tradition.

He presently lives in Brighton Ontario and maintains a studio and gallery there called Gallery 96. Andrew is now retired from St.Lawrence College as Curator of the Marianne van Silfhout Gallery and Fine Arts Professor and Faculty Advisor to focus exclusively on his art and workshop practice.

Andrew has also taught at The Albright Knox Art Gallery, Durham College, The Varley Art Gallery, Thousand Island School of Art, Loyalist Summer Arts Programs and The Cedar Ridge Art Centre.

Andrew is also the Executive Director of ArtVentures , Director of the Markham School of Fine Art, Prince Edward County School of Art, and the Peggy's Cove School of Fine Art.

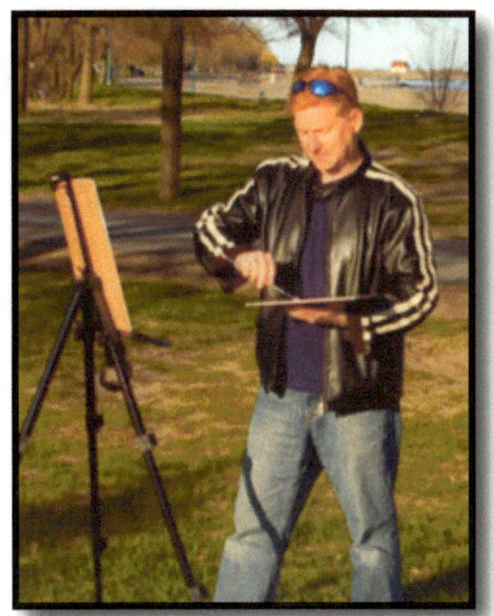

Website – http://andrewhamiltonfineart.weebly.com/

Instagram – https://www.instagram.com/andrewhamiltonart/

Google business listing –
https://www.google.ca/search?q=art+galleries+brighton+ontario&btnK=Google+Search&source=hp&ei=jFSuYc6KHIy7tQbpyp64Dg&iflsig=ALs-wAMAAAAAYa5inLvwVwOHu5hCVzA7ySPu-3yqUPPF&ved=0ahUKEwjOgPGM5c_0AhWMXc0KHWmlB-cQ4dUDCAo&uact=5&oq=gary+v+mar-keting+2021&gs_lcp=Cgdnd3Mtd2l6EAMyCAghEBYQHRAeOgsIABCABBCxAxCDAToRCC4QgAQQsQMQgwEQxwEQ0QM6CAgAEIAEELEDOggILhCxAxCDAToOCC4QgAQQsQMQxwEQ0QM6BQgAEIAEOg4ILhCABBCxAxDHARCjAjoICC4QgAQQsQM6CwguEIAEELEDEIMBOgUILhCAB-DoLCC4QgAQQxwEQrwE6CAgAEIAEEMkDOgYIABAWEB46CAgAEBYQChAeULMPWIhtYLJwaABwAHgAgAGoAogBvhySAQYwLjE1LjeYAQCgAQGwAQA&sclient=gws-wiz

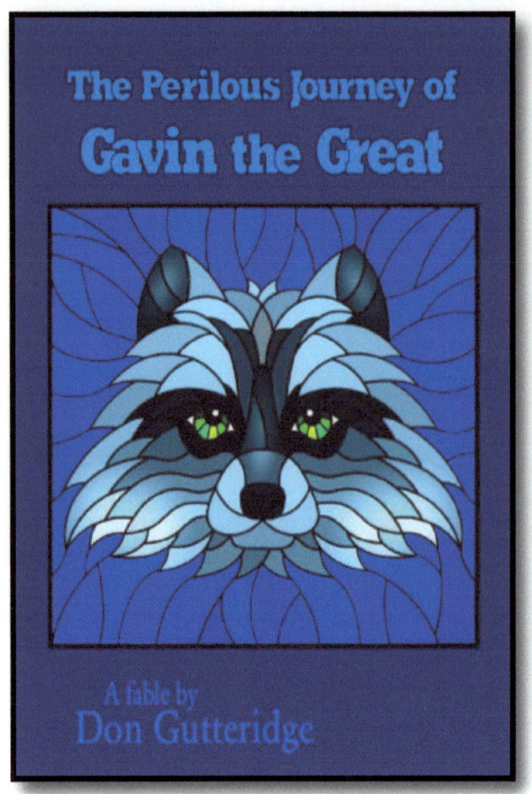

Available on Amazon.ca, Amazon.com
and other eStores around the world.
Also available at www.WetInkBooks.com

A Perilous Journey of Gavin the Great

A middle-grade novel, a fable about a raccoon who tries to guide his animal brethren home after disaster strikes. When Gavin awakens on a fallen tree trunk, the raccoon is certain the catastrophic flood that hit Earthwood was only a nightmare. But it really happened, and that trunk has likely been floating aimlessly for some time. Luckily, he soon finds his brothers, Trisbert and Cuyler, as well as other "woods-creatures," including rabbits, mice, and a snake. When they finally get an inkling as to where they are, they realize getting back to Earthwood will be an arduous trek—through the predator-filled Forest of Everdark. Gavin, the oldest grandson of Earthwood's "clan coon" head, becomes the flood survivors' leader. They're in danger of terrifying foes, from wolves and coyotes to "universally evil" Tallwalkers who wield lethal "firesticks."

Courage is a must, but they'll need brains as well to safely cross bodies of water and outwit predators that would otherwise devour them. All the while, they can only hope their missing friends and families are waiting for them.

Gutteridge's gripping novel is often dark; threats against the woods-creatures are constant, and not everyone makes it to the end. It's nevertheless exciting as Gavin and the rest overcome obstacles in their path and enemies (like a fox) form alliances. What little humor there is comes courtesy of the woods-creatures' interpretations of humans, who speak "Gibberlish" and drive "doomsmobiles." These animals constitute a huge, appealing cast, including Gavin, a great commander in the making, and the porcupine Quiver, who either uses words incorrectly (a noble sediment) or simply makes them up (temcrestuous). Along with charming nods to Scripture and literature, from the biblical story of Noah and the flood to the Knights of the Round Table, this journey delivers a handful of surprises, particularly an effective final-act twist.

A riveting morality tale with a marvelous forest-dwelling cast.

Kirkus Book Review

The first pararaph of the after word by Brian T. W. Way

Gavin's Search for the Golden Quail

The spring rains have come to Earthwood but, with them, disaster. For these rains do not stop. They continue to fall and fall, becoming a flood, a catastrophic deluge. It may be an after-effect of the Great Burning in the neighboring nation-state but, whatever the cause, a great wave of water now rises and rises and begins to sweep away all of the civilization that the wise young racoons of Earthwood have ever known. Earth melts into swamp, trees topple into ruin and a dense fog rolls across the land, all but decimating this land of the Ring-tails. The only escape, to rush to the high ground of Serpentine Ridge and broach the border of Everdark, but that is no escape at all, for in that direction lies certain death at the hands of fierce predators and whatever other evil might exist beyond. Gavin, the oldest of three brother-racoons, all separated from their father and the other elders of the clan, knows that his survival and that of his brothers, Trisbert and Cuyler, is his respon-sibility. He has to become their leader. He has to rely on his abilities and on the wisdom he can recall and enact from lessons given to him from The Book of Coon-Craft and his training as next RA-to-be. But the situation is so dire, so uncertain, and the fog so thick…

Poetry Canada

Poetry Editor: Bruce Kauffman
Photo Editor: Richard M. Grove

Bruce Kauffman
"Poetry Canada" Editor

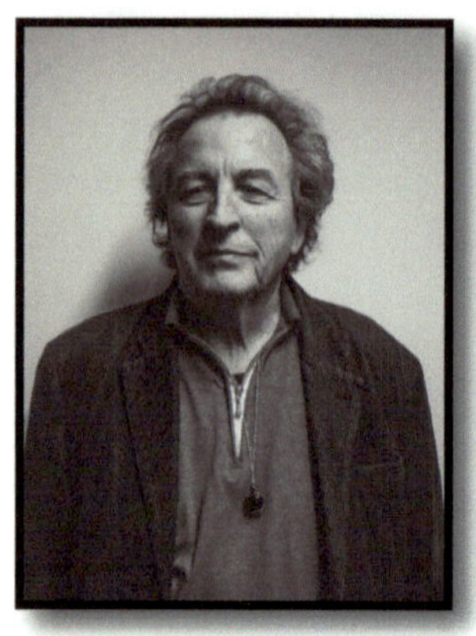

Bruce Kauffman lives in Kingston and is a poet and editor. His latest collection of poetry, an evening's absence still waiting for moon, was published in 2019. He facilitates intuitive writing workshops, and hosts the monthly and the journey continues open mic reading series begun in 2009, and also produces & hosts the weekly spoken word radio show, finding a voice, on CFRC 101.9fm he began in 2010.

time

these molasses days

roll by

      time almost
      frozen in itself

this slow motion
of what becoming
      is

return

to shut down half
        the sound
half the noise

there is too much
of it
in this hour
        this place
for me to absorb

i say
shut it all down
half again
then again
and again
        again
        again

over and over
to the point
i can once more hear
the breath
        and faint whisper
        of a dragonfly

there

i believe there
        is a forest
on the other side of
        this wide lake

i listen to the language
of the birds

they tell stories
of a vast forest
on water's other side

perhaps their stories
are poetry
and mean also
        something else

perhaps their stories
are music   an old song
a song so old
        before even those trees
almost as old as water
and their melody sprouted
a first tree there

perhaps their words
are a dream
a visioning
perhaps the trees
        are simply mirage

perhaps this water
before me
and even i
are illusion instead

Amanda Murgel
amuggle23@yahoo.ca
Toronto, Ontario

The Story of Eden

Six women,
          A circle of them within a circle of green
Held still in their dance.

This is our glimpse into
          that lost garden
Kept guarded by these bodies,
          their sea-black hair and
          gentle, calloused hands
that ebb and flow in dance and hold each other

Created not from a rib
          but a stroke of orange, green and peach

There is no snake, there is no tree.

Anna Nieminen
climatejusticefitness@gmail.com
Scarborough, Ontario

#NoFitnessOnASickPlanet

Like so many fitpros
I did a pandemic pivot,
offered branded virtual classes
for domestic goddesses,
suggested isolation was like service
to family and community,
cringed later when I heard
newscasts about the covert covid abuse,
while women's organizations taught the
violence at home signal for help.

Tried offering a series about personal alchemy,
a routine about owning our thrones,
but when our mentor sat on hers for a photo,
it was a mirror to my own white privilege;
over-worked front-line workers
don't have energy for fitness,
can hardly take the weight off their feet.

Then the heat dome that killed over 600 people
and baked billions of sea creatures in their home,
the fire that swallowed a village
consumed in 20 minutes,
The wild winds, the flooding,
a stirring in my gut,
my heart ached, my breaths were shallow,
I couldn't stomach marketing those classes,
Eco-anxious indigestion   moved me.

Now I strengthen my
climate justice core values with a twist,
full-body reach overhead
to stretch my eco-consciousness,
symbolize holding the Earth in my hands,
make intentions for climate action
and breathe, *breathe*.

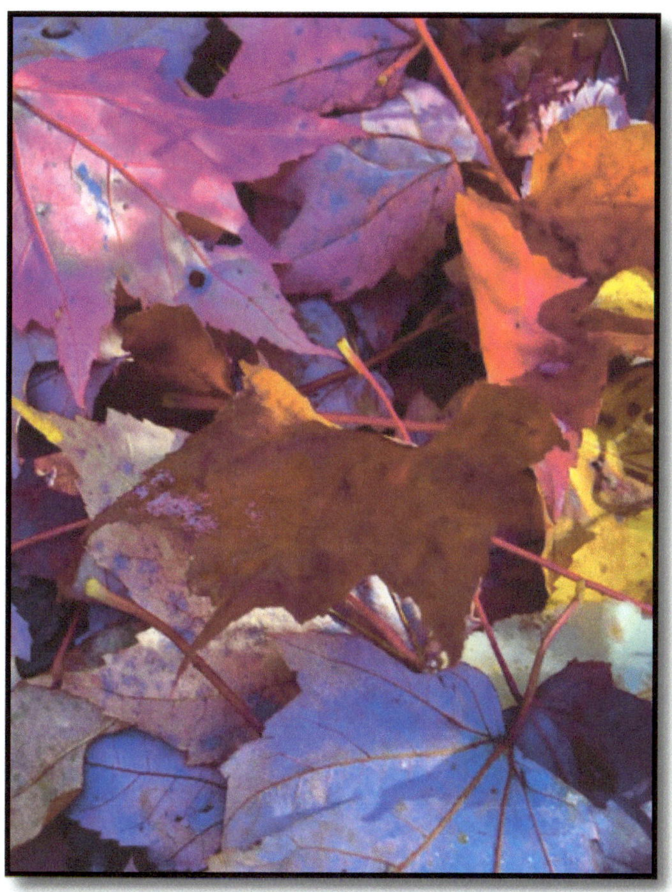

Ann Di Nardo

Anne Archer
tannii@hotmail.com
Sharbot Lake, Ontario

Rivers, 2022:
Big Lake Festival, Cold Creek Vineyards

We enter the barn and walk
past the open piano and the score,

its torrent of notes
and rests, handwritten

on paper the size of a folio
so that the turning of a page

makes the surface ripple. Light filters
through spaces and gaps, the sun

sets in bands of rose as
the soloist takes us upstream

through white water to shallow pools
to the river's source. We are carried

by whatever guides her
fingers—quicksilver like late August

dusk over bails, stooks
and stubble. We roll up

our pant legs, step into her river.

Breanna Habinski,
s29322@rmc-cmr.ca
Kingston, Ontario

A Portrait of a Pair of Fair Things

Why do you blush at me
My fair portrait of a lady?
Is it because
I can see through the cracks in your paint
Laid so bare
With wear and tear?

Nay, nay
I beg of thee
Fear not my wandering eyes
They undress you not.
Rather they address
The careful strokes
Which made you look down your nose
At me so sharply

Alas
On passing we
Could not pass a word
Yet your vibrant oils speak to me still
They holler sweet nothings at me
As I cruise by
Chastely averting my gaze
From your illuminous
Voluminous
Big, bold, white, motherly
Pearls

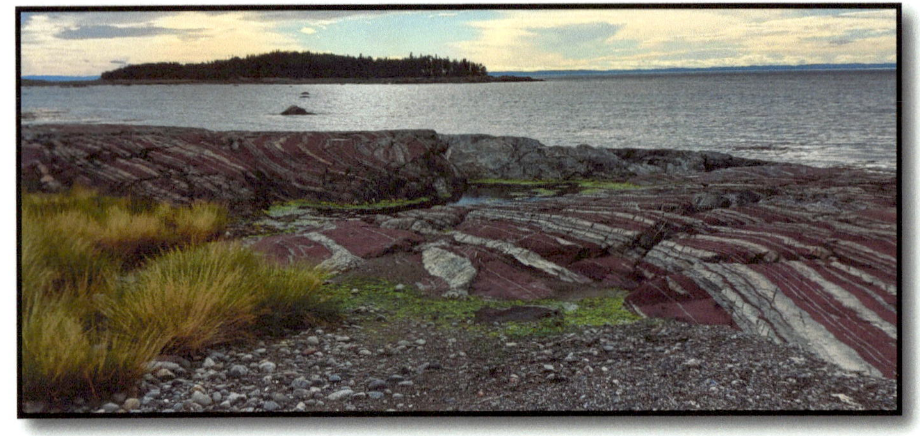

Françoise Romard
Trois-Pistoles, QC pre-sunset

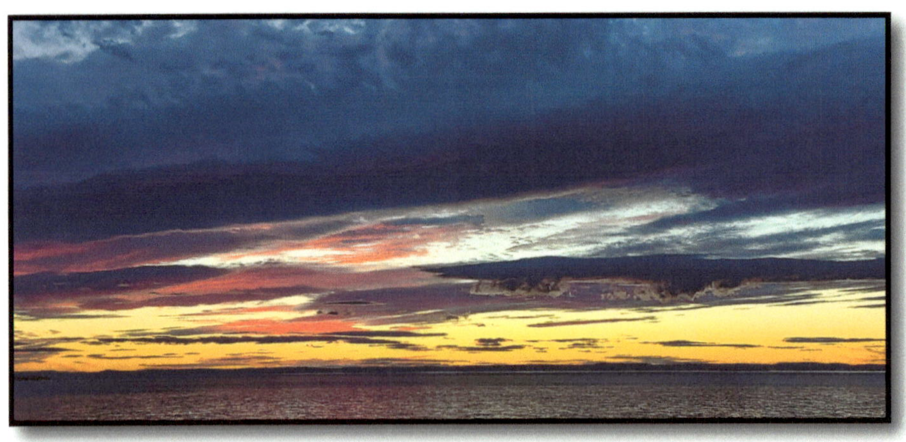

Françoise Romard
Trois-Pistoles, QC sunset – 01

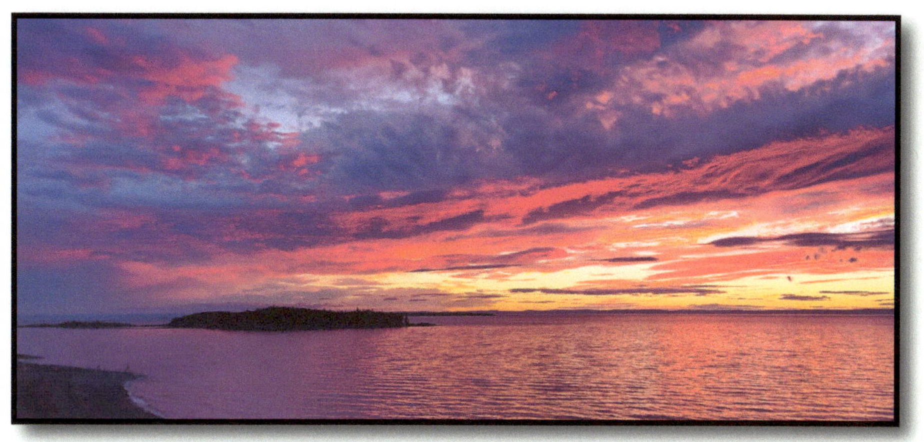

Françoise Romard
Trois-Pistoles ,QC – Sunset – 02

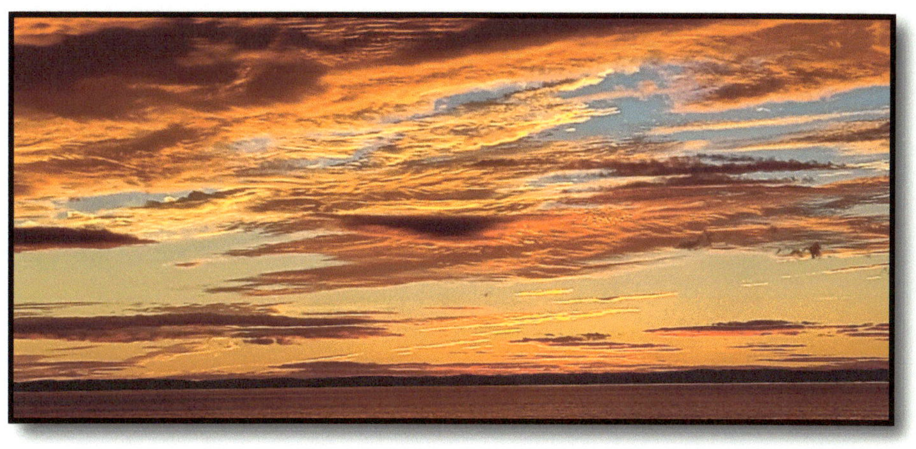

Françoise Romard
Trois-Pistoles ,QC – Sunset – 03

Courtney Townson
courtney.townson0626@gmail.com
Kingston, Ontario

Poor Unfortunate Soul

Prickling hot pain stabs itself into the plains of her feet
with every step,
as though stomping on glass.
Pain is a small price to pay
to carve and saw away
at the body until it fits.
To mimic the mould
in the tabloids and the mirror,
until the person looking back is
a stranger with one of those faces
you swear you have seen before.
Years of youth washed away by words of contempt
sitting on her preened puckered lips.
The innocent calf stolen from her home,
slaughtered and prepared to please the palate.
She has lost. Her worth
determined by the waist of her jeans
that bare her anxiety in inches.

Suck it up, try to make those numbers fall –
fall like the tears from her eyes at midnight
when nobody is watching,
her only rebellion against the inescapable gaze.
She would speak, but who would listen?

Based on the original tale of "The Little Mermaid", where a mermaid trades her voice for legs to chase after a man she is in love with. With every step on her human legs, it feels like stepping on swords. She is unable to make him fall in love with her, as he marries someone else, and the little mermaid dies.

D. Le Doan
phung7170@gmail.com
Beaconsfield, Québec

Spring Rain

Trees and bushes in bare forms are reaching up
beyond their earthly confines. They're on a new
fulfilling journey.

The supporting ground rises up from its long
frozen position to welcome the rain:
I haven't seen you for a long time.

The clear-eyed window brushes away
the hindering raindrops that crawl
on its eyes like insects.

Ed Woods
edwoods26@hotmail.com
Dundas, Ontario

Chinook Break

Dust settled
then coated everything
but my mind

A poem can be created
in the worst of conditions
Use a pencil in this case
for dust clogs a pen tip

Alberta Badlands Chinook
rusty particles in the wind
swirl came to a stop
pipeline construction restarts

I see the beauty of earth
in this barren landscape
no longer a bandit's hideout

My work is completed for now
several minutes to wait
then back to its cycle again
but now secondary work starts

Writing pad and pencil out
the pipe is my current table
sunlight is better than any lamp

Elaine Yu
elaine.yu@lifetech.com
Toronto, Ontario

Autumn Possession

Flatten the body, with the tail
connected in a straight line, lying down
on the fence wall under sunlight. Not moving at all.

I figured he must have completed this year's
        autumn possession,
who used to run back and forth with a green fruit
        in his mouth, slipped past me,
turned around a few times, and
moved to the bottom of a hidden birch tree.

Wrapped in a warm wool coat,
and disguised as his kind-
soft, cunning, alert,
while watching him sleep. You tell me

how to get ready for
the food of the whole winter, and deepen into
        the nest of dreams,
with the whole season,
listen, singing like in a dream.

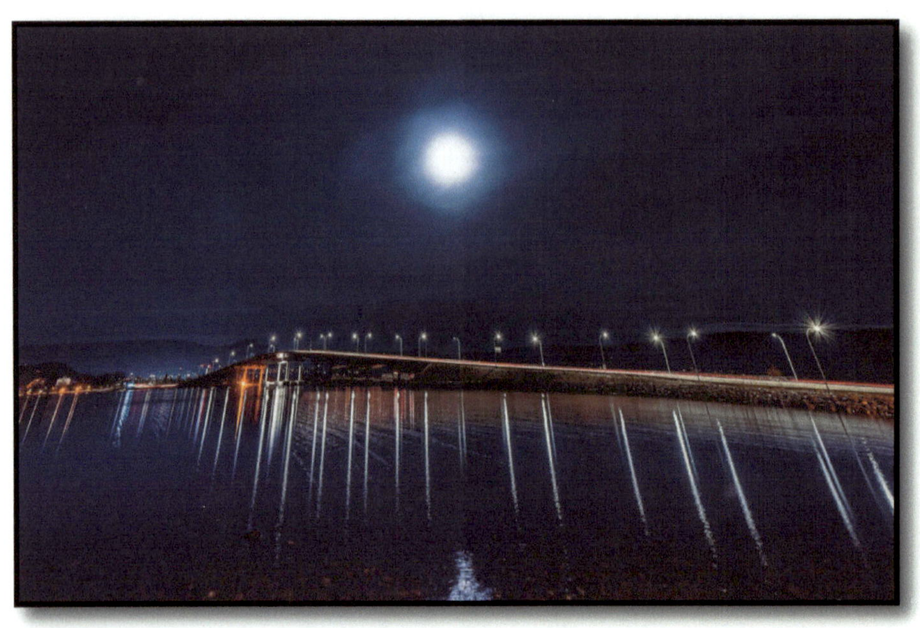

Yanive Feiner
Kelowna Bridge

Yanive Feiner
Nelson Bridge

Joseph A Farina
jfarina@cogeco.ca
Sarnia, Ontario

dune dance

we never danced on the beach
only walked leaving moonlit footprints
eyes open for cherry topped cruisers
hunting curfew criminals from
weekend teenaged assignations
cruising the shadows of canatara
silent among the others
hearts and breath tripbeating
as we spoke words
"that had just the right amount of letters.
just the right sound"*
stolen from the top ten charts
to prove that ours was forever

we never danced on that beach
but i did with you at home in my room
writing in journals that you would never see
danced barefoot whispering in your ear
words that were mine and just for you.

**from 'Cherish' by The Association*

Julia Brousseau
julia-brousseau@hotmail.com
Kingston, Ontario

When We Were Birds

When we were birds, we moved without sound
only breath,
the purple sinew of muscle flapping our wings.

The air was our stage.
We danced among the clouds,

You flew and
flew.

Arcing upwards, downwards
whizzing past one another.

Without breath we would be nothing.

We did not know where we were,
only that we were free.

We held together,
a flock of wonder
light beaming through clouds

we soared, in those days.

Purple shimmer of wings in the sunlight,
still catches my eye.

Just like light hitting a stone

    thrown into the water

        we
          shone.

Lee-Ann Taras
leeanntaras@kos.net
Kingston, Ontario

This Is a Loss That Cannot Be Spoken

my grief is so vast it is guttural
a mournful howl released from depths below in the belly
throat choaking on sobs of infinite tears
this is true anguish,
relentless and brutal
like the smacking of sorrow
at my father's death
I cried myself dry then
plunging into the bowels of that dark, December's night
I had never known such grief,
immense, immediate and with an intensity
that burned like acid
it left me hollow, empty
inconsolable, alone with my love
there is another side that comes with such great sadness
the eventually found peace
of a daughter once loved,
the gifts of remembering and acceptance,
the imprint of our ancestors on our pulsating hearts,
rich with blood and history
brimming with a love,
endless and eternal
in this we are truly immortal
and grateful
a love given lives on
long after skin and bone becomes ash

Patrick Connors
patrickjt.connors@gmail.com
Toronto, Ontario

Kingston Road in the 1980's

Three slices of moist bread cut diagonally
layers of bacon, lettuce, and tomato –
this is when they put mayonnaise
on a BLT, or at least Miracle Whip.

French fries scooped out of a plastic tub
always cooked a little less or a little more
than you would have preferred, topped
with pepper and salt and saltier gravy.

A can of lukewarm Coca Cola foaming
over the rim of a parfait glass filled
with so much ice it took at least
three pours to drink it all.

Or a cup of coffee, the third one of the day–
the equalizer, the source of fake energy,
which sat in the pot for over two hours–
and needed three teaspoons of sugar.

Mini jukeboxes within an arms length
asked only for the quarters you didn't spend
at the video arcade, so you could play a song
and tell your friend it was your favourite.

Teresa Hall
thallartist@gmail.com
Scarborough, Ontario

The Arctic

'A strange beauty, this world of blue ice.'
A white bear-shape is swimming effortlessly
alongside huge sculpted forms, caught in
the incandescent light hanging between
silvery sky and sea; at one with these sentinels
guarding this windswept bay. Storms are
forming, crossing far flung heights, then mists
carry over into long winter's night.
Bearded ones circle their young near
rock-strewn slopes, as dark shadows lope
across this rippled landscape. Quick footsteps
fall as a lone fox steals lemming morsels
dropped by a great snowy owl. An arctic tern takes
flight above the scree with laughter following, as
Inuit children run breathlessly along the shore.
This is also the land of the endless day…

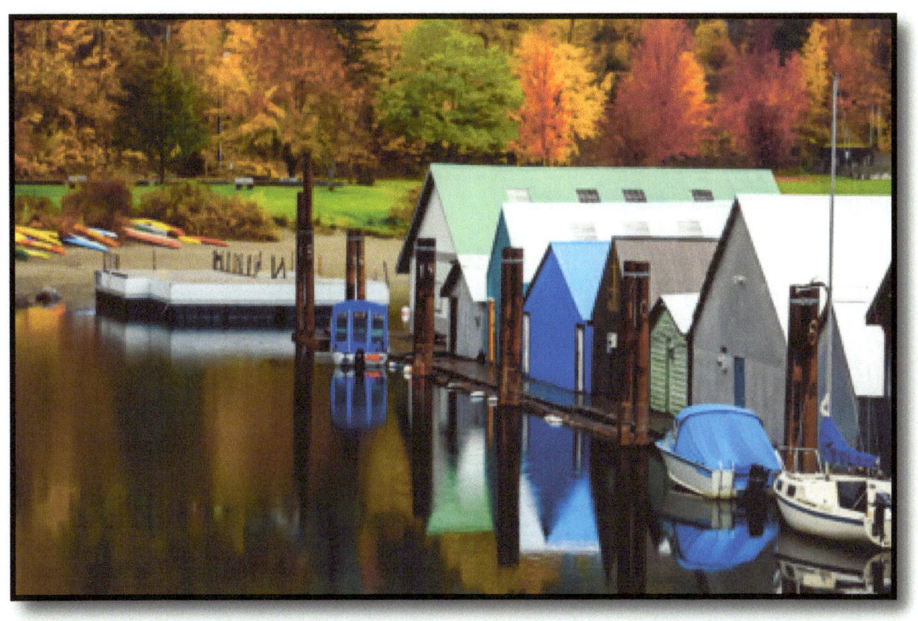

Yanive Feiner
Boat House

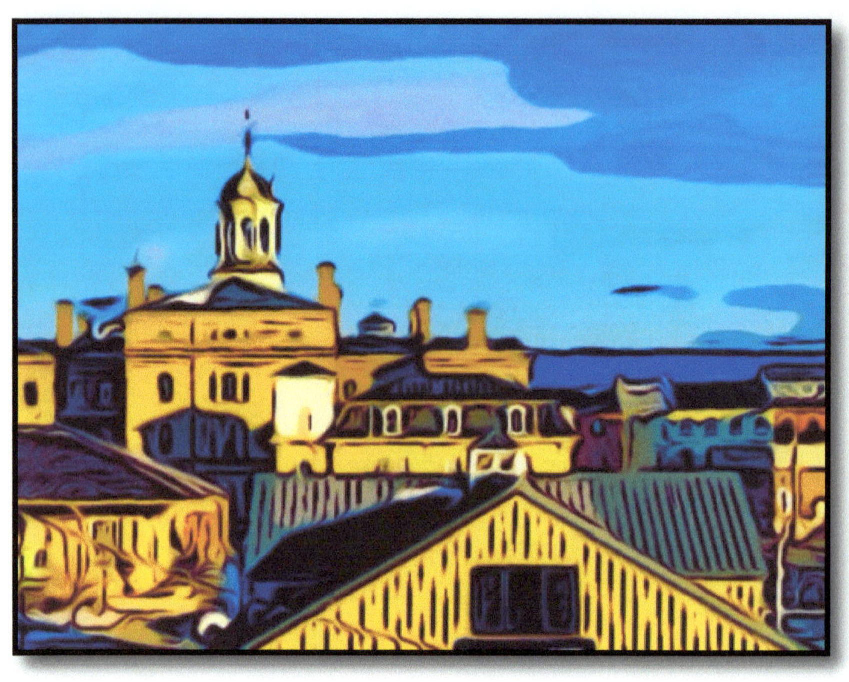

Cobourg 01 and 02 – Ann Di Nardo

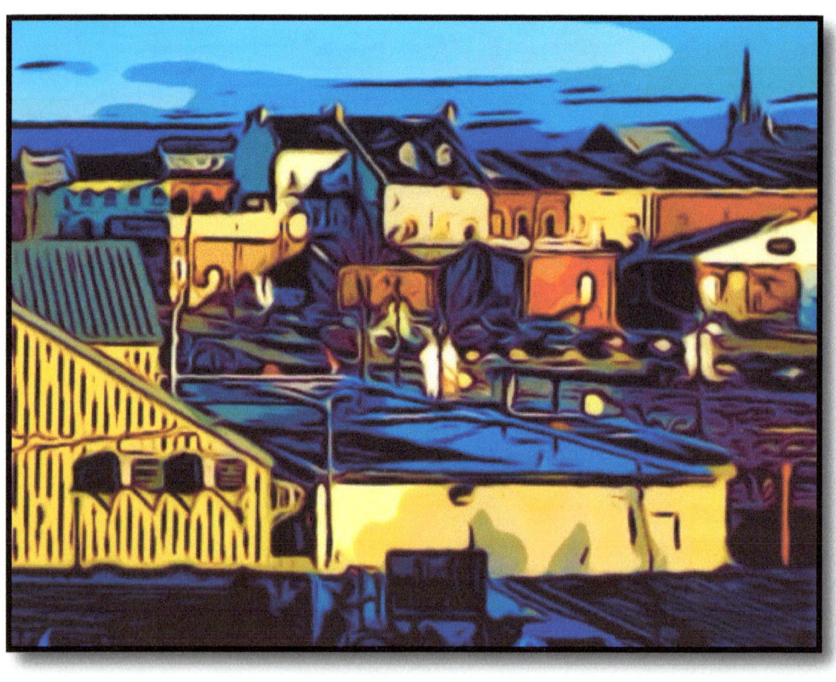

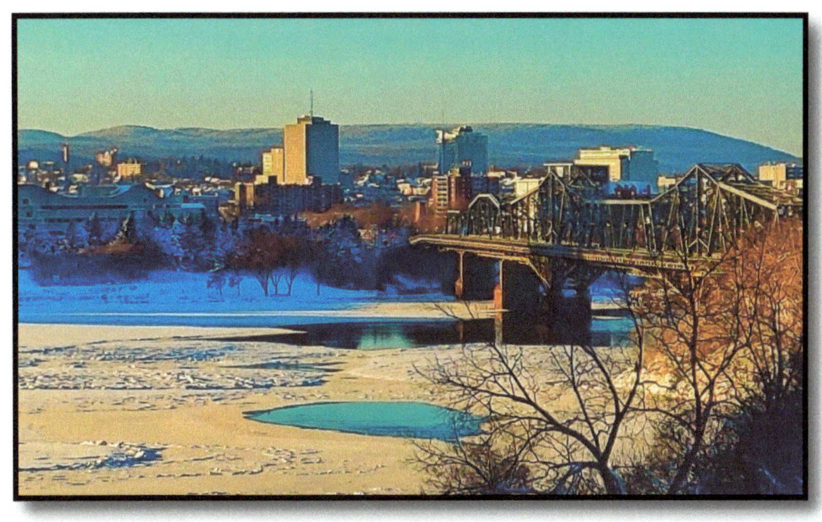

The view from Ottawa across the Ottawa River
Richard Marvin Tiberius (Tai) Grove

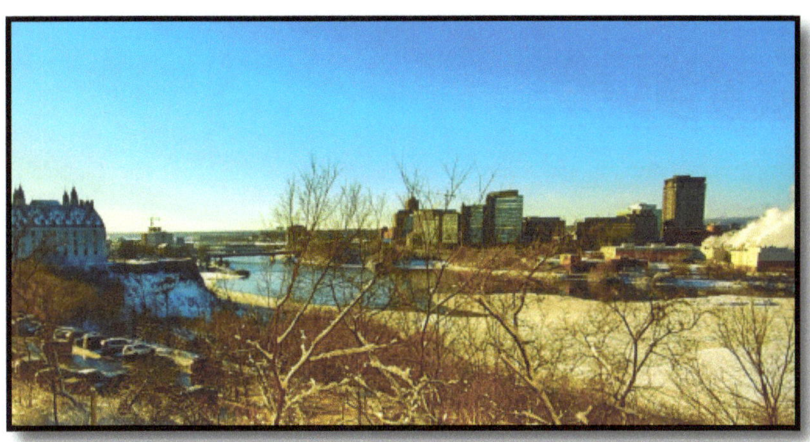

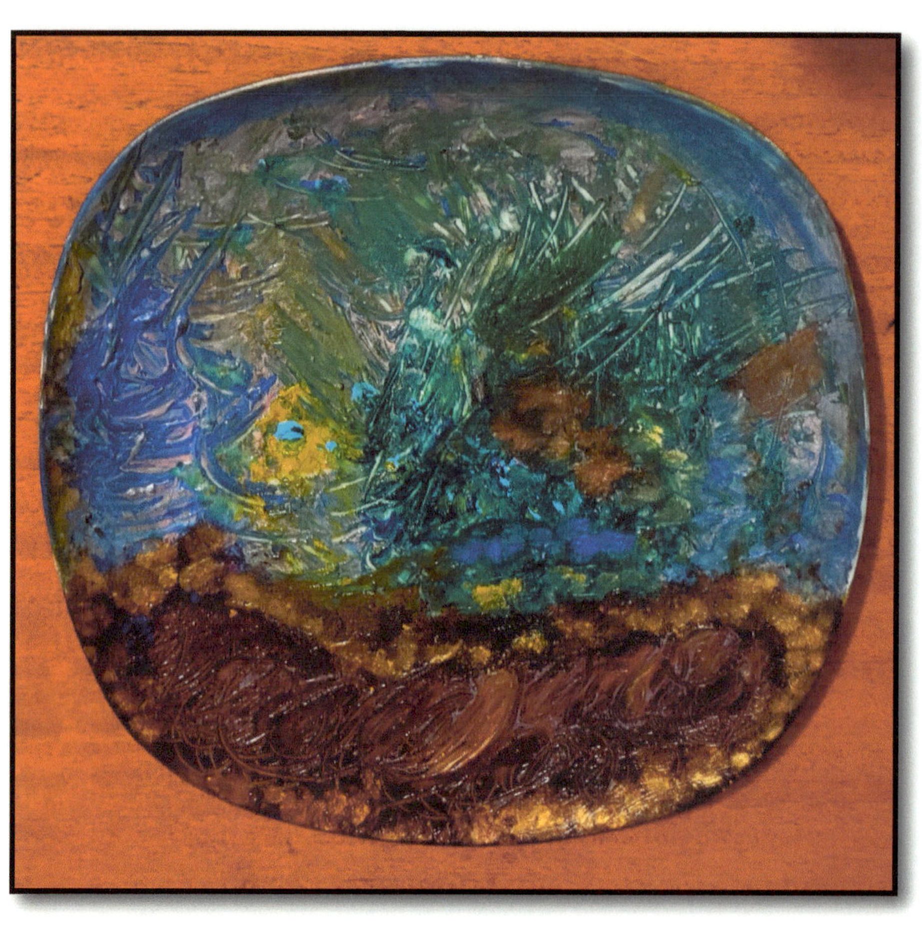

Anna Panunto
The Flat Painted Dish-Plate

Anna Panunto <antod@sympatico.ca>

The Flat Painted Dish-Plate

(for your 80th birthday in heaven daddy)

Daddy, you and I are the deep orange sunset;
perfectly divided
almost like two golden halves of a full moon.
Let me remain the center of your solar system,
even if we can no longer rise and set together.
When the Sun goes past its 18 degrees below the horizon,
whisper a prayer for all of humanity.
I still mirror your reflection each waking day.
They say that you live inside my smile
and my voice echoes fragments of your spirit.

Daddy, I still drink from your favorite wine glass.
I touch its translucent stem and imagine
your charismatic laugh,
and, on those special anniversaries
of birth and death, I still eat from your favorite dish-plate
yet, this flat white vessel is no longer pleasing to my eyes.
Its ugly with deep scratches etched at its center
reminds me of the shallowness of life.
So, I painted it.

Daddy, the dish-plate has now become ceremonial.
As I was painting it, with all five fingers
our story magically became imprinted on it.
Its varying shades of burgundy, maroon, and crimson
paying homage to our ancestors.
My fingers, are now channeling me
into another dimension,
just as I am deliciously blending deep blues with gold.
My spirit is dancing with you now.
We are perfectly tuned to the dance of Creation.
The circular movements of my fingers
have now finished the story.
And, the dish-plate is ready...
Until we meet again, Daddy.